RABB

RABBITS
The Key to Understanding Your Rabbit

Virginia Parker Guidry

**photographs by
Reneé Stockdale**

CompanionHouse Books™ is an imprint of Fox Chapel Publishers International Ltd.

Editorial Director: Christopher Reggio

Photos: PonomarenkoNataly/Shutterstock: 26; DenisNata/Shutterstock: 48;
Cora Mueller/Shutterstock: 58; Stocklite/Shutterstock: 144, 162
All other photos copyright © 1998, 2001 by Stockdale, Inc.

ISBN 978-1-62008-145-7

The Library of Congress has cataloged an earlier printing as follows:
Guidry, Virginia Parker.
  Rabbits/Virginia Parker Guidry;photographs by Renee Stockdale.
    p. cm.
  ISBN-13: 978-1-889540-73-3 (paperback : alk. paper)
  ISBN-10: 1-889540-73-0 (paperback : alk. paper)
  1. Rabbits. I.Title.
  SF453 .G85 2001
  636.9'32--dc21
                                        2001001329

This book has been published with the intent to provide accurate and authoritative information in regard to the subject matter within. While every precaution has been taken in the preparation of this book, the author and publisher expressly disclaim any responsibility for any errors, omissions, or adverse effects arising from the use or application of the information contained herein. The techniques and suggestions are used at the reader's discretion and are not to be considered a substitute for veterinary care. If you suspect a medical problem, consult your veterinarian.

Fox Chapel Publishing
903 Square Street
Mount Joy, PA 17552

Fox Chapel Publishers International Ltd.
7 Danefield Road, Selsey (Chichester)
West Sussex PO20 9DA, U.K.

www.facebook.com/companionhousebooks

Printed and bound in Singapore
21 20 19 18   10 9

ACKNOWLEDGMENTS

I'm grateful to the knowledgeable rabbit enthusiasts who were willing to answer my many questions, especially Jeffrey R. Jenkins, D.V.M., of the Avian and Exotic Animal Hospital in San Diego, CA. And thanks to the House Rabbit Society and the American Rabbit Breeders Association—two wonderful resources for all rabbit lovers.

—V.P.G.

I would like to thank my new friend Sandy Griggs of Sandy's Royal Angoras, Warren, MI; Amy Williams of Williams' Rabbitry, Milford, MI and her children, Lauren, Christopher, and Ashley, for supplying bunny models for this book; Dr. Simon of Woodside Animal Hospital, Royal Oak, MI; Pet Stop of South Lyon, MI; Melissa Danley; Nancy, Joey, and Nikki Mitts; Erika Strausberg; April Moore; Marti and Myia Blackwood; Diane McIntyre; Sheila Wiggins; and Jill Wells.

A special thanks to my son, Jerid, who is dearly loved and to our own bunnies, who are always patient with me.

—R.S.

CONTENTS

CHAPTER ONE

Long Ago and Far Away: Rabbit History

Rabbits are super pets. Ask any bunny owner. Rabbits are cuddly, quiet, full of personality, affordable, fairly small, and they get along well with other pets. And they're really cute and really soft. These are all good reasons why domestic rabbits are popular companion animals—and probably why you just acquired (or are considering acquiring) a rabbit.

Rabbits haven't always enjoyed a super-pet status, though. Only since the last quarter of the twentieth century have rabbits been considered popular pets. That may seem strange, considering how common it is today to own a pet rabbit. It's not unusual to know someone who has a rabbit, to see rabbits for sale in a pet store, or to see rabbit supplies advertised in the newspaper. Rabbit publications are easy to find at the library, and information about rabbits is available on the Internet. It's even common for schools to have a classroom bunny.

But long ago and far away, the domesticated rabbit's ancestors were wild creatures. Rabbits experienced none of the benefits or problems associated with domesticity. At several points in history, rabbits were kept, bred, coaxed, befriended, and tamed. Countless generations later, we have a fabulous house pet.

Their long ears, wiggly nose, soft coat, humorous antics, and ability to hop-hop-hop have captivated and endeared us. It doesn't matter whether rabbits are placed in a work of literature or a drawing, or admired in the wild or as house pets. We can't help but love and exclaim over them.

Rabbits often are portrayed as heartwarming, playful characters in children's stories.

Children's author and animal lover Beatrix Potter intui-tively knew the rabbit's appeal and chose Peter Rabbit to star in her stories. *The Tale of Peter Rabbit*, originally based on a letter Potter wrote in 1893 to the young son of her former governess, was an instant success. And it still is successful today. Readers young and old continue to enjoy the antics of Peter Rabbit—along with other bunny tales written by Potter such as *The Tale of Benjamin Bunny* and *The Tale of the Flopsy Bunnies*. Exactly what is it about these stories that makes them so popular? Undoubtedly they're exiting, well written with colorful illustrations (drawn by Potter), and fun. They also have happy endings. Most likely, though, the tales owe their popularity to Potter's primary choice of animal character: the rabbit.

Children's classics aside, the domestic rabbit has been a close companion of humankind for many generations in a variety of ways, some not so pleasing to lovers of companion animals. Traditionally viewed as a source of food and fur, and used as a lab animal, the rabbit has most recently—in the last twenty years—achieved the status it really deserves: special companion and house pet. Today's domestic rabbit is almost as popular as the cat and dog. Nutrition, care, and training information is readily available, as are products and foods specially made for rabbits. No longer just an Easter pet, the rabbit enjoys all the benefits (and sometimes heartbreaks) of popular companion animals.

Wild Beginnings

Today's domestic rabbit, in spite of breed differences (color, size, shape, and fur), can be traced back to one wild species: the European wild rabbit, or *Oryctolagus cuniculus*. Although there are about twenty-five species of wild rabbits throughout the world, only *Oryctolagus cuniculus* has been domesticated. Rabbits, along with their wild cousins, hares and pikas, are members of the Lagomorpha order of mammals. Rabbits were once classified as rodents, but rabbits, hares, and pikas are not rodents (order Rodentia) even though they share a few characteristics such as ever-growing teeth. Unlike rodents, rabbits have two sets of upper front teeth.

All domesticated rabbit breeds are descendants of the European wild rabbit.

Did You Know?

The word Lagomorpha is derived from the Greek words *lagos*, which means hare, and *morphe*, which means form or shape.

A rabbit's teeth grow continuously.

Historians speculate that early civilizations recognized rabbits as a potential food source and hunted rabbits for meat. As to the rabbit's origin, several sources point to southwestern Europe, in Spain, where caves contain pictures of rabbits dating from the Stone Age. Fossil remains show that rabbits lived in this area for thousands of years. Although controversial among historians, it is believed that rabbits in Europe and Africa were used for meat and fur around 600 B.C., but there isn't much recorded history prior to the Roman civilization.

The seafaring Phoenicians of the ancient world (1100 B.C.) also recognized rabbits as a valuable meat source and traded them throughout the known world. In fact, one of the first written accounts about rabbits is attributed to the Phoenicians. Ten centuries later (100 B.C.), rabbits were introduced to Italy, as recorded by the Roman scholar Varro. Again, rabbits were considered a valuable food source and were kept in enclosures. These semidomesticated animals were most likely imported throughout the Roman Empire, and the rabbit achieved a notable status: rabbit images were imprinted on Roman coins issued during the reign of Emperor Hadrian (sources vary, but approximately 120 A.D.). And some historians note that Romans developed a longhair rabbit at this time—the Angora—with long, fine hair perfect for spinning into yarn.

Rabbits were introduced to the British Isles around 1066, following the Norman Conquest. Following that, the mention of rabbits can be found in writings from the twelfth and thirteenth centuries, mostly as food sources to the wealthy who kept the semidomesticated animals in enclosures.

Rabbits took a leap toward true domesticity during the Middle Ages. Kept by French monks, rabbits were considered a food source for monks and for visitors to the monasteries. Rabbits were also prized for their fur. They were kept in hutches and bred for a variety of colors. Through selective breeding—and within the protective walls of the monastery—the monks produced color varieties not found in the wild.

Selective breeding continued to grow during the next few centuries, with new varieties of rabbits with differing colors and sizes being developed. At the beginning of the eighteenth century, there were seven distinct breeds. A century later, the number of breeds increased to twelve. Paintings from the seventeenth and eighteenth centuries depict rabbits we now know as Netherland dwarfs and Polish. But rabbit enthusiasts can thank breeders from the eighteenth and nineteenth centuries for the incredible variety of rabbits available today. It seems that during this period of industrial revolution, breeding stock, whether it was horses, dogs, or rabbits, became a highly competitive hobby. The idea of breeding rabbits solely for meat was out. Breeding to improve, add, change, or astonish was in. The rabbit fancy, including breed standards, breed clubs, national organizations, shows, and good breeding practices, was born. The first true domestic breed was the English lop, characterized by large, floppy ears.

The fur color of wild rabbits is called agouti.

One of the first rabbit clubs to form in Great Britain was the Metropolitan Rabbit Club, which began attracting fanciers in 1845. The British Rabbit Council started up in 1934 and still exists today. In the United States, The American Rabbit Breeders Association (ARBA) was formed in 1910; it still exists. Both organizations oversee many aspects of the rabbit fancy, including showing, public education, commercial use, standards, and registration.

The once wild, then semiwild, rabbit is now fully domesticated, living intimately with people. But though the domestic rabbit shares his life with the human species, he is still a rabbit, complete with the natural behaviors and unique physiology found in wild rabbits.

Only domesticated rabbits, such as the lop, have ears that droop down rather than stand up.

Did You Know?

The years 1898-1901 are known among rabbit enthusiasts as the "Great Belgian Hare Era" because of the great popularity of the breed.

As prey animals, rabbits use their senses of sight and hearing to always be on alert for danger.

The rabbit is muscular and compact with powerful hind legs. He is a sensitive creature, with a sharp sense of hearing and smell. He can turn each ear independently to pinpoint the faintest sound, and his nose has one hundred million scent cells. His eyes, which give him great peripheral vision, are large and endearing. Rabbits see best in low light conditions, not in bright sunlight, which is a good thing since rabbits are most active at dawn and dusk.

The rabbit's ears—oh those characteristic ears—stand tall or, in some modern domestic breeds, flop. Rabbits have a dense coat of fur, naturally brown-gray in the wild, a tail that resembles a cotton ball, and furry feet. They are a fabulous creation, handsome and carefully crafted.

In the wild, the rabbit is a prey animal, which is why he needs such large hind legs: to escape. Rabbits move quickly. In open land, a wild rabbit can reach a speed of 24 miles per hour. Another way the rabbit escapes the prospect of becoming dinner is by burrowing and hiding underground; his front legs are well suited to digging.

Wild rabbits live in a community (usually eight to fifteen colony members) of safe burrows called a warren. The wild rabbit doesn't venture too far from his underground habitat, 500 yards or so, to ensure safety and security from predators. Naturally, the rabbit is a cautious animal and is constantly on the lookout for danger.

A wild rabbit usually ventures out from his underground home at dawn and dusk and commences eating. Every day, rain or shine, rabbits eat their fill of wild grass and other edible greenery.

Top right: The hind legs of a rabbit are powerful and allow him to quickly hop to safety should a predator appear. Bottom right: As a burrowing animal, a rabbit's front legs are especially suited for digging.

Both wild and domestic rabbits groom themselves constantly.

The rabbit's reputation for the ability to multiply quickly is based on fact. With a gestation period of four weeks, litters averaging four to five for wild rabbits, and sexual maturity being reached at six months of age, it's not long before a warren must be expanded for new members. A healthy female averages three litters a year. Pregnant females usually do not remain in the community burrow during gestation but dig a special nesting burrow nearby. This is because male rabbits are often aggressive toward the young and may even kill them.

Rabbits are good housekeepers. They keep their burrows neat and tidy by urinating and defecating in one place, usually away from the burrow. Rabbits are also meticulous groomers: they lick and scrub themselves frequently.

A habit wild rabbits carried with them into domesticity is coprophagy, ingesting their own fecal matter. However disgusting it seems to owners, the act is completely normal and healthy in pet rabbits. Rabbits produce two kinds of fecal pellets: the normal hard one, and soft ones that are usually expelled at night. The soft pellets are the result of prolonged digestion: movement between the cecum and the large intestine and back again. These pellets are rich in protein and B vitamins and add important nutrients to the rabbit's diet. This is a normal part of digestion, and rabbit owners need not be alarmed.

To people, rabbits are extremely quiet creatures, and this is true in the respect that they're not very vocal. Rabbits, wild or domestic, have plenty to say—in their own language. They are social creatures who communicate with each other via quiet sounds and postures. Rabbits communicate through body language or by making sounds such as purring.

Rabbits are territorial creatures with a distinct pecking order in each colony. Each family has an alpha buck (un-neutered male) and alpha doe (unspayed female), with lower ranking males and females under them. Though generally peaceful animals, rabbits will fight if the social order is disrupted, for example if unfamiliar rabbits try to invade the colony.

It has been said that domestic rabbits have changed little since their wild days, in spite of generations of breeding and in spite of the unnatural circumstances in which pet rabbits live today. Domestic rabbits have retained much of their original wild character—physiology, behavior, temperament—which is probably why we find them such fascinating animals. No longer considered primarily a food or fur source, the rabbit is a beloved pet. As such, the rabbit deserves the best care we can offer.

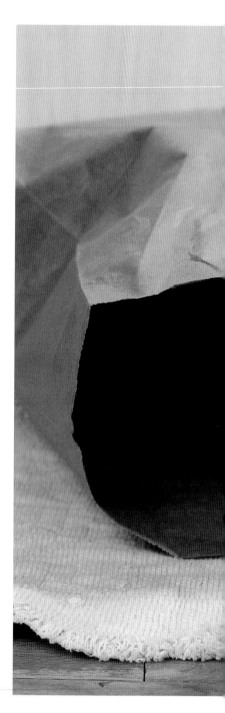

Rabbits are playful.

CHAPTER TWO

Is a Rabbit the Right Pet for You?

RABBITS ARE FRIENDLY COMPANIONS AND INTERESTING animals. Rabbit enthusiasts say there's no better pet. But in spite of the rabbit's positive characteristics—cute, fun, friendly, easy to keep—a rabbit isn't the pet for everyone. This has nothing to do with the rabbit, of course, and everything to do with the potential or new rabbit owner—you.

So how do you know if a rabbit is the best choice of pet for you and your family? Let's take a look at the unique friendships that exist between pets and people. A special relationship called the human-animal bond exists between people and companion animals. Rabbits, dogs, cats, birds, and other small mammals often become best friends to their human keepers, giving love and companionship unconditionally. The devotion is reciprocated, and most pet owners will do anything for their pets. Pets are considered family members with many domestic rights and privileges. They are enjoyed when present, worried about when ill, and grieved over when deceased.

Though in the past rabbits were primarily valued for their meat, fur, or breeding purposes, they are also now beloved companions. People have discovered that rabbits, like dogs and cats, can be devoted friends: rabbits make us laugh, soothe our nerves, ease our loneliness, and give us purpose. There's a special bond between people and rabbits, just as there is between people and other companion animals. Owning a rabbit means making a commitment to a special relationship. It's a step that should be taken carefully, with a great deal of thought. Too many people rush into adopting or buying a pet and end up wishing they hadn't. Don't be impulsive no matter how cute the bunny is!

Responsibility

First and most important in deciding if a rabbit is a good pet for you is determining whether or not you are willing to accept responsibility for a rabbit's care. (Of course, this applies to any pet.) Can and will you commit to providing care for the duration of a rabbit's life span, which can be anywhere from five to ten years, depending upon the breed? (Small breeds usually live longer than large breeds.) That responsibility means daily feeding and hutch or cage cleaning, providing veterinary care, exercising, grooming, and spending time with your rabbit. It means making a financial investment and an investment of your time in an animal who is totally dependent on you. What a rabbit needs most is a committed, responsible owner. Can you offer that? If the answer is yes, should you feel free to rush out and acquire a rabbit? No, not yet. There's more to consider.

Before buying a bunny as an Easter gift, think about whether the recipient can responsibly care for that pet for five to ten years.

Cost

The good news about rabbit ownership is that it's not terribly expensive compared to owning other companion animals. The purchase price of a purebred rabbit averages $20–50, annual minimum costs are $50, and rabbits are fairly healthy animals, which means veterinary bills (other than spaying and neutering) are usually low. On average, expect to spend about $125 a year on caring for a rabbit.

The bad news is that potential owners—of any companion animal—rarely count the costs before bringing home a pet. Too often, owners are surprised at how much it costs to properly feed, house, and care for an animal and end up dumping that pet at a shelter. Or, an owner is already saddled with debt when he or she acquires a pet and the pet becomes ill, ringing up hundreds of dollars in vet bills. The owner believes giving up the pet is the best option. Another common scenario is the big-hearted animal lover who already has, say, four cats, three dogs, two rabbits, a bird, and an iguana and brings home a stray he or she finds at the park. The person's not sure how he or she's going to pay for another animal, and the others may suffer because there's a limited amount of money to cover pet costs.

The best news is that it doesn't have to be bad news when it comes to pet care costs. After asking yourself if you're willing to be a responsible rabbit owner, ask yourself another simple question: can you afford a pet? Be honest! If your financial status is questionable, a pet is probably not a good idea—at the present time. Pay off debt, set up a budget, and start a savings plan for buying a pet. After all that, then go ahead with the purchase.

Rabbit ownership requires an initial investment for items such as a cage, a litter box, some food, bowls, litter, grooming tools, toys, and others.

Common Costs

Purchase price (purebreds)	$20-50
Shelter adoption fee	$50-100
Small mammal cage	$35
Hutch	$25-100
Water bottle	$5
Food dishes	$5-15
Rabbit care book	$10-20
Litter pan and scoop	$20
Pellets	$50 a year
Spay or neuter operation	$50-200
Petsitter	$15-25 a night

Costs may vary among pet supply retailers, so shop wisely.

Are You a "Rabbit Person"?

Though it hasn't been documented scientifically, animal enthusiasts attest to the fact that people with certain personalities are attracted to certain companion animals. There are "rabbit people," "cat people," "dog people," and "bird people." In other words, some people enjoy the company of, and are naturally drawn to, a certain species. And there are those who enjoy a variety of pets. But in many cases, owners are single-minded in their devotion to one species. What does this have to do with owning a rabbit? Plenty!

Before you consider bringing home a rabbit, ask yourself if you're a "rabbit person." (There's nothing mysterious about this term, and it doesn't mean that you prefer vegetables or have big ears.)

If you're a "rabbit person," living with a rabbit is a rewarding experience.

In other words, do you really like rabbits? Do you enjoy their antics? Do you appreciate the species? Do you understand, or wish to understand, their natural behaviors? These are important questions to ask yourself. The answers should all be *yes*. There's no sense in adopting an animal species that you don't enjoy. Let's face it: we all have favorites when it comes to pets. There's nothing wrong in that. What's important is knowing yourself well enough to know which animal species you like best.

It's essential to consider your lifestyle when evaluating if a rabbit is a good pet match for you. How much time can you devote to a pet? Do you leave the house to go to work or school all day, or are you home? A rabbit fits into a working person's lifestyle quite well, according to the House Rabbit Society, a nonprofit organization dedicated to rescuing and caring for rabbits. Because rabbits are most active at dawn and dusk, they spend the midday—the time an owner is usually away from home working or at school—napping or sitting quietly.

Do you travel frequently? A rabbit, especially one kept as a house pet, requires time and attention. Rabbits are social animals and get lonely if left to themselves too much. If you are away from home a lot and would need to board your pet or hire a pet-sitter frequently, a rabbit, or any pet, may not be a good idea.

Where do you live, and how do you plan to house a rabbit? Will she live inside as a house pet, outdoors in a hutch, or a little of both? A house with a yard or shed is ideal if you plan to keep the rabbit in a hutch. An apartment or house is fine for a house bunny. If you rent, be sure your landlord allows pets.

Do you have children and if so, what ages? Don't expect a child to be responsible for the rabbit's care. As far as responsibility, no child should ever be expected to be a primary caregiver. Caring for any animal is an adult responsibility. Rabbits are delightful pets and can be dear friends to youngsters. Most experts agree, however, that rabbits are not suitable pets for children under seven years of age. A rabbit's delicate physical and sensitive nature (remember, they're prey animals in the wild) combined with a toddler's commotion and clumsy motor skills can spell disaster, usually for the rabbit.

Are you an active hiker, camper, or jogger? Do you want a pet who will accompany you on outings? If so, get a Labrador retriever, not a rabbit. While you may be able to train your rabbit to "walk" on a leash for a hop around the neighborhood, don't expect her to jog next to you while you ride a bike or accompany you on a mountain hike.

Are there other pets in the household? Rabbits are sociable creatures and get along with other animals, including cats and dogs, but rabbits can be aggressive about their territory. Dogs and cats are natural predators who could instinctively harm or even kill a rabbit. Interspecies introductions must be done slowly and carefully, and interactions thereafter should always be closely monitored.

As you can see, there are many lifestyle factors that determine whether a rabbit is a good pet for you. Evaluate your lifestyle carefully before you make a decision. Now that we've taken a good look at you, the potential rabbit owner, let's take a closer look at the rabbit.

Breed

There are forty-five rabbit breeds recognized by the American Rabbit Breeders Association. Breeds come in a variety of sizes. Colors and coat patterns are seemingly endless, as are temperaments.

Consider your children's ages and maturity before acquiring a rabbit.

Prospective owners have a multitude of choices when it comes to picking a purebred rabbit. The decision is enough to make one's head spin.

Which breeds or mixed breeds make the best beginner's pet? Well, that depends upon whom you ask. Every breeder, rabbit enthusiast, and veterinarian has an opinion—and they're all different! That's very confusing to prospective owners. But most experts do agree on the following advice for first-time rabbit owners: get what you like. Choose a breed that appeals to you because then you will take better care of the rabbit. Each breed has unique qualities that appeal to different individuals. There's a breed for everyone. Beyond choosing what appeals to you, keep in mind size (more on that later), fur (some breeds such as wool breeds require more grooming), and temperament (which isn't necessarily determined by breed).

Given proper introductions
and time, your other pets
may get along famously
with your rabbit someday.

Breeds

Once you decide to adopt a rabbit, you have the tough task of determining which breed you want. They're all so beautiful! Listed below are the forty-five breeds of rabbits recognized by the American Rabbit Breeders Association.

American
American fuzzy lop
American sable

Angora, giant
Angora, satin
Belgian hare
Beveren
Britannia petite
Californian
Champagne d'argent
Checkered giant
Chinchilla, American
Chinchilla, giant
Chinchilla, standard
Cinnamon
Creme d'argent

Dutch
English spot
Flemish giant
Florida white
Harlequin
Havana
Himalayan
Hotot
Hotot, dwarf
Jersey wooly (below)
Lilac
Lop, English
Lop, French
Lop, Holland
Lop, mini
Netherland dwarf
New Zealand
Palomino
Polish
Rex
Rex, mini (left)
Rhinelander
Satin
Silver
Silver fox
Silver marten
Tan

Lops can look comical.

Personality

Don't be fooled by the rabbit's gentle and quiet nature. Underneath that understated composure is an intelligent, fun-loving, playful animal with unique likes and dislikes.

Temperaments vary: some rabbits are easygoing, others are nervous. There are rabbits who enjoy being held and rabbits who prefer soft stroking. Some are easy to train to use a litter box, others more difficult. Some are timid, some bold. Some rabbits enjoy the company of other rabbits or animals, others prefer having an owner all to themselves.

Can you expect certain temperaments from certain breeds? Some experts say *yes*, some say *sometimes*. Others believe a rabbit's attitude and temperament depends more on how she is treated, rather than her breed; all rabbits can be wonderful pets if they're treated kindly.

The moral of the story? Even rabbits of the same breed are individuals, with unique and differing personalities. Get acquainted with a rabbit before bringing her home. That way you will understand her personality and temperament and will be able to judge if you're a good match.

Size

Not only do rabbits differ in temperament but they're available in a variety of sizes: dwarf, small, medium, and large. It's important to understand size when considering a pet rabbit. Large rabbits can weigh up to 20 pounds while dwarf rabbits weigh a dainty 2 to 3 pounds. Obviously, space, housing, and feeding requirements vary depending on a rabbit's size.

The Netherland dwarf weighs only 2 to 3 pounds.

A rex rabbit has a dense, velvety coat.

The tiniest rabbits, called dwarf rabbits, are just like any other of their species, only they are smaller. Dwarfs are popular pets with individuals who have limited living space: a small apartment, for instance. The Netherland dwarf, Himalayan, Polish, and Britannia petite are a few dwarf breeds.

Small rabbits, who usually weigh about 4 to 7 pounds, are also popular. They are large enough to be handled but are not too heavy. The Dutch, tan, Florida white, and mini lop are small rabbit breeds.

About half of all rabbit breeds are medium size, weighing 9 to 12 pounds as adults. Many breeds in this weight size are or were produced for meat. Medium-size breeds include the New Zealand, the French and English lops, and the rex.

The largest rabbits are considered giants, and when compared to the tiny 2-pound dwarf, a 16-pound rabbit is just that! The Flemish giant is considered the world's largest rabbit breed; the checkered giant and giant chinchilla (the chinchilla breed is different from the animal of the same name) also tip the scales. Though large, giants are generally characterized as docile and lovable.

Some rabbit enthusiasts recommend large rabbit breeds only if owners have plenty of space, preferably a fenced yard in which the rabbit can hop about. Without proper exercise, a rabbit will become obese and lethargic.

Other Physical Characteristics

Along with being considered one of the oldest domestic rabbits, the English lop has a unique characteristic not found in wild rabbits: ears that flop instead of stand up. When choosing a rabbit breed, consider which ear "style" you like best. Some people enjoy the comical, friendly look floppy ears give; others prefer the traditional stand-up ears.

Most rabbit breeds have fur that is categorized as normal, which means it is about 1 inch long with a fine, soft undercoat. Another type of fur, rex fur, is found only on rex rabbits. With short, plush, extremely soft fur, the rex is considered "king of the fur." Satin fur is characterized by a small-diameter hair shaft and a more transparent hair shell than normal fur. The transparent nature gives the fur intense color and luster. You can't miss breeds with angora fur: the hair grows 2 to 3 inches in length and gives the rabbit a sheeplike appearance. The fur, also called wool on breeds such as the English and French Angoras, can be harvested (plucked or sheared) and spun into yarn.

Shorthair breeds require little hands-on grooming from owners. Wool breeds, though, are labor intensive, requiring brushing or combing at least three or four times a week or even every day.

Male or Female

Some rabbit enthusiasts believe males make the best pets, others advocate females. Both sexes make excellent pets, but they do have their differences, especially if they have not been neutered or spayed. Bucks have a tendency toward aggression and spraying urine to mark territory. Does are preoccupied with nesting and rearing young, which means they can be somewhat aloof. As long as you're not planning on breeding, the best plan is to spay or neuter your rabbit. Altering rabbits, as long as it's done when the rabbits are fairly young (four to six months for does, and three to four months for bucks), minimizes sexual behaviors, resulting in males and females being equally good pets.

The Angora
and other wool
breeds require
extra grooming.

Beginner's Tips

If you're a first-time rabbit owner, consider the following tips:

- Learn as much as you can about rabbits and their care before acquiring a pet rabbit.

- Begin with one rabbit if you've never kept rabbits before.

- Consider getting a small breed, one that weighs 4 to 7 pounds. Small rabbits are popular first-time pets. They are easy for beginners (both adults and children) to handle and are not too delicate.

- Shy away from challenging breeds such as wool breeds (they require a lot of grooming) or dwarfs (they're delicate and sometimes nervous).

- Choose a healthy rabbit.

- Purchase your rabbit from a reputable breeder, or adopt her from a rabbit rescue group.

- Locate a rabbit-savvy vet.

- Be aware that popular breeds can be prone to more health problems.

- Join a local rabbit club.

- Get a breed you like.

CHAPTER THREE

Adopting a Rabbit

Ready, set, adopt a rabbit! But from whom or where? That's a good question, considering how important it is to acquire a healthy animal. So, if you're absolutely sure a bunny is the pet for you, here's how to find and select one. There are four main ways to attain a rabbit: buy from a breeder, adopt from a shelter, purchase from a pet store, or acquire from an individual.

The Breeder

Rabbit breeders breed rabbits, right? Then contacting a reputable breeder is an obvious choice when acquiring a rabbit. There are many ways to find a breeder in your area: Ask for a referral from the American Rabbit Breeders Association (see appendix for address), ask your veterinarian or a friend who owns a rabbit for a breeder's name, post a request on the Internet at an animal forum or site, or attend a rabbit show.

It may take some effort to find a good local breeder, but some rabbit enthusiasts believe buying from a breeder is the best way to obtain a healthy animal at a good price. First, a reputable breeder knows and understands rabbits. He or she is an invaluable resource to a new rabbit owner, from helping an owner choose a breed to making suggestions on how to care for the animal once he's home. Buying a rabbit from a breeder helps ensure that the animal is healthy, too. Whether for business or hobby, a reputable breeder takes pride in a well-maintained rabbitry with healthy animals. If you buy from a breeder, you'll know specifics of the breed and exactly how big the rabbit will be when he matures. For example, a satin breeder is able to tell you that satins are medium in size, weighing 9 to 10 pounds at maturity; that the breed is docile, with an easygoing temperament; and that the satin's hallmark is his incredible fur. Such information helps you determine whether a particular breed is really the one you want.

The Shelter

Public interest in rabbits as pets is proof positive that popularity has a price. Sadly, rabbits have joined the thousands upon thousands of companion animals routinely dumped at shelters. Some owners who no longer want rabbits release them into the wild under the mistaken assumption that domestic rabbits can live on their own. They usually don't survive in the wild, given such dangers as dogs, cats, cars, and malnutrition. That's the bad news.

The good news is that animal shelters and rabbit rescue organizations are dedicated to finding good homes for these abandoned rabbits. That means, prospective rabbit owner, that

The Reputable Breeder

Unfortunately, not everyone who breeds rabbits is quality conscious. Do business with individuals whose animals reflect quality care, thoughtful breeding, and genuine concern. Otherwise, you may purchase an unhealthy animal—and help keep someone in business who shouldn't be.

- A reputable breeder enjoys, appreciates, and loves both rabbits in general and the particular breed(s) he or she fancies.

- A reputable breeder is knowledgeable about rabbits and about his or her particular breed(s).

- A reputable breeder's rabbits are healthy and well tended.

- A reputable breeder's rabbitry is clean, well maintained, and suited to the rabbits' needs.

- A reputable breeder is, or has been, actively involved in the rabbit fancy (clubs, shows, judging, etc.).

- A reputable breeder is willing to help potential owners determine whether a particular breed is the right pet or show stock for the buyer and is willing to help new owners learn to care for their pets properly.

animal shelters or rescue organizations are a great place to find adoptable rabbits. Not only can you obtain a lovable pet but you may even save a life!

Look in the yellow pages under animal shelters or humane societies to find shelters in your area. Give an organization a call to find out if rabbits are available. If not, ask to be placed on a waiting list or ask for a referral to another shelter. Also, contact the House Rabbit Society (see appendix for address) for local volunteers with rabbits awaiting adoption.

Just because you're adopting doesn't mean you get a free rabbit. Most shelters require an adoption fee or a nonrefundable donation. Give it willingly! Animal welfare organizations are known for operating on shoestring budgets with funds frequently coming from the volunteers themselves. Shelters and rescue organizations also screen prospective owners and ask them to sign an adoption agreement. (These vary but usually require owners to spay or neuter an animal or return the animal to the organization should they decide to relinquish him.)

If you're not particularly fussy about the breed, sex, or age of a rabbit, adopting is a great way to become a rabbit owner. If, however, you have your heart set on a certain breed or if you wish to show your rabbit, it's better to contact a breeder.

Pet Store

It seems like there's always a bunny in the window at a pet store. In fact, pet stores are an easy and convenient place to find a rabbit, and you can buy supplies at the same time. Shopping at a pet store has a few drawbacks to carefully consider, though. Stores usually stock only the most popular rabbit breeds, which means if you're looking for an unusual breed, you probably won't find it at a pet store. Sometimes pet stores also stock mixed-breed rabbits, who make fine pets. But it's sometimes difficult to estimate how big a young mixed-breed rabbit will be at maturity if the rabbit's heritage is in question. Pet store clerks are not always rabbit experts, so you can't depend on them for accurate information. It's a good idea to take your new bunny for a veterinary checkup if you buy him at a pet store.

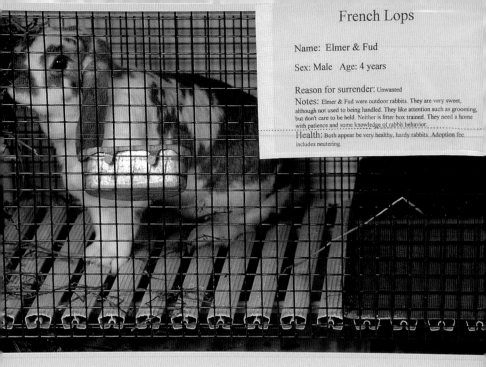

French Lops

Name: Elmer & Fud

Sex: Male   Age: 4 years

Reason for surrender: Unwanted

Notes: Elmer & Fud were outdoor rabbits. They are very sweet, although not used to being handled. They like attention such as grooming, but don't care to be held. Neither is litter box trained. They need a home with patience and some knowledge of rabbit behavior.

Health: Both appear be very healthy, hardy rabbits. Adoption fee includes neutering.

Above: If age or breed isn't important to you, consider buying your rabbit at an animal shelter. Below: Most pet stores carry a limited variety of rabbit breeds.

Individual

You may acquire a rabbit from an individual: a neighbor who is moving, a coworker who impulsively buys a rabbit but discovers her landlord won't allow pets, a friend who's doe just had a litter, or someone advertising a rabbit "free to good home" in the newspaper. This can be a great way to acquire a pet because you may actually be doing that person—and rabbit—a favor by adopting the animal. Another plus is that the rabbit may be free, and the individual may throw in a few supplies. But, again, be sure to take your new pet to a veterinarian for a full checkup.

You may meet someone who can no longer care for his or her rabbit and is looking for a good home for the pet.

Just like adopting a rabbit from a shelter, acquiring one from an individual is a gamble: the rabbit could be young, old, small, large, or any breed. Again, if owning a particular breed with a pedigree is important, contact a breeder.

Now that you know where to acquire a rabbit, the next consideration is choosing an individual. While this may seem easy, it can be a little tricky. First, pick a healthy, active rabbit. Avoid a rabbit who appears listless or depressed. His eyes should be bright and free of discharge, as should his nose. Check the insides of the front legs for matted fur (this results from a rabbit wiping a runny nose, so it's not a healthy sign). Look inside the ears to make sure there is no brownish waxy residue, which can indicate ear mites. Make sure the hindquarters are clean and free from signs of diarrhea. A healthy rabbit's droppings are round and hard. Overall, the rabbit's body and fur should be clean and odorless.

Check the rabbit's front teeth. The upper and lower teeth should come together evenly, and the top teeth should not overlap the bottom. When this occurs, it's usually due to a congenital defect called malocclusion or "buck teeth." It can be a problem. Because a rabbit's teeth grow continuously, they must meet evenly in order to be ground down naturally. Otherwise, they continue to grow and eventually prevent the rabbit from eating at all. Choose a rabbit with straight teeth that meet evenly.

If your heart is set on raising a baby rabbit, called a kit, he should be no younger than eight to twelve weeks of age when you bring him home. This will ensure his health and safety. The kits of some large breeds require that they spend more time with the doe before separating.

Remember that rabbit personalities vary. You want to choose a rabbit with whom you are compatible and whose company you will enjoy. When visiting a rabbitry, shelter, or pet store, pay careful attention to each rabbit. (What you see is often what you get!) Observe how the rabbits interact, and observe how each rabbit responds to human interaction. Ask yourself: *Does the rabbit seem playful and sociable, or is he somewhat timid? Does the rabbit respond to handling? Does he enjoy being petted?* Pick a rabbit with a personality you like.

Ask the seller if a pedigree is available. A pedigree is a registry recording a line of ancestors of three generations or more. If you're not planning on showing or breeding, a pedigree is not essential. But if you are, you'll need those papers.

Now that you've read all this information on where to find a pet rabbit and how to choose a healthy one, get busy searching. The fun is just beginning!

Put a lot of thought into choosing a rabbit who is right for you.

CHAPTER FOUR

Preparing for a Rabbit

Now that you know where to find a rabbit, you're probably itching to bring one home. But first you've got to lay the groundwork for a good owner-pet relationship. That means you must prepare yourself and your home for the rabbit's arrival. First, you must decide whether you want a house bunny or if you want to keep the bunny outside. Then there are housing considerations, safety precautions, supplies to buy, family introductions, and shopping for healthful food, just to name a few. So why not brew yourself a cup of tea, sit down, and read what's to follow.

Indoors or Outdoors?

Not too long ago, rabbits were kept in backyard hutches. Period. But along with the rabbit's new status as house pet come a few new ideas about keeping rabbits. Rabbits are still kept outdoors in hutches, of course, but they also live indoors as pampered house pets, roaming about (supervised!) yet confined in cages or small rabbit-proofed rooms when necessary. Or, rabbits are kept outdoors in hutches during mild weather, indoors when it's over 80 degrees Fahrenheit, raining, or snowing. Some rabbits enjoy outings on a leash or in a small, fenced "pasture" in the backyard.

As you can see, the idea that a rabbit should be housed only in a backyard hutch no longer rules rabbits and their owners. What this means for you, the prospective rabbit owner, is you must decide if you want a house rabbit, an outdoor rabbit, or a little of both.

If your rabbit lives indoors, she is more likely to become a member of the family.

If you live in a climate where there are extremes in temperatures, your rabbit will be healthier if kept inside the house during hot and cold weather.

The House Rabbit Society encourages all owners to keep rabbits indoors as house pets, and the advantages of doing so are many to both owner and rabbit. First, given the rabbit's subtle nature, some enthusiasts believe it's impossible to truly enjoy, appreciate, and understand a rabbit if you don't keep her inside your home. Keeping her as a house pet is the best way for owner and rabbit to get acquainted with each other—and develop a close bond. Keeping a rabbit inside also ensures her safety, as long as an owner properly supervises her. Rabbits kept outdoors in hutches are vulnerable to attacks from predators (neighborhood dogs, roaming cats, and wildlife) and experience stress from weather changes. Like a dog or cat, an indoor rabbit enjoys the cozy protection a home can provide.

Owners who keep their rabbit indoors are more likely to notice signs of illness, making it easier to keep track of the animal's health. Disease symptoms are often subtle in rabbits, so it can be difficult to tell if a rabbit is sick, especially if you keep your rabbit in an outdoor hutch and don't see her but once a day when you visit her. But if your rabbit is a constant indoor companion, it's more likely that you, the owner, will notice if something is amiss. Last, but certainly not least, keeping a rabbit indoors is fun and enjoyable. House-bunny advocates can't say enough good things about sharing their domain with rabbit friends. Once you give it a try, you'll never regret it!

Many rabbit enthusiasts and breeders still keep rabbits in outdoor hutches, and that may be an option if you do not wish to keep the rabbit indoors. Outdoor rabbits have special needs of which you must be aware, however.

Keeping your rabbit indoors will help you keep in touch with your rabbit's likes and dislikes.

They must be carefully protected from the elements (sun, wind, heat, rain) and from predators. That means buying or building a well-constructed hutch. Don't skimp! A hutch is an outdoor rabbit's only protection. You must also make sure that a hutch rabbit gets plenty of exercise and social interaction (solitary confinement is lonely for the social rabbit), and you must keep the hutch clean.

There are zoning ordinances to consider when keeping rabbits outdoors. Check with local city or county government to make sure that rabbit keeping is legal in your area. And even if it is, you may encounter disagreeable neighbors who don't care to live next door to a rabbitry, however small.

Indoor Housing

Will your bunny live primarily indoors or outdoors? The type of housing you buy hinges on this decision. If you're planning to keep your rabbit indoors with supervised outings in the house, a wire-sided cage (mesh no larger than 1 inch by 2 inches) with a removable, washable pan is a good choice. This provides an indoor rabbit with a private hideaway and a place you can confine your pet safely when necessary. Buy a cage made especially for rabbits; it should have a large side opening for easy access.

The cage should be large enough so the rabbit can stretch out and hop about (roughly six times the length of the full-grown rabbit; she should be able to stand up on her hind legs without her ears touching the top. There should be plenty of room for a litter box, a sleeping area, and food containers. Obviously, the necessary cage size will vary among breeds, so use common sense when choosing a cage.

Buy a cage that is large
enough for the rabbit so
she can stand up on her
hind legs.

The cage flooring for an indoor cage can be either wire mesh or solid. Owners who litter train their rabbits usually choose solid plastic or rustproof metal floors. (There's really no need for a wire bottom if the rabbit uses a litter box.) Wire flooring is acceptable, though, as long as it's smooth and galvanized. The floor should be made of approximately 1-inch by 1½-inch mesh. Be aware that wire can be irritating to a rabbit's feet, so you must provide a place in the cage where a rabbit can rest off the wire bottom. Some owners place a small piece of wood (do not use redwood, which is toxic to rabbits) or a blanket on the floor.

Many experts recommend placing a nest box in an indoor rabbit's cage, especially if other pets or children live in the house. A nest box is a small cubbyhole in which you place bedding. Since rabbits are naturally burrowing animals, a nest box provides a rabbit with a sense of security. Most nest boxes are made of wood and can be purchased anywhere rabbit supplies are sold. A nest box should be large enough that the rabbit can turn around when there are several inches of bedding inside the box. The entrance should be large enough so the rabbit can come and go with ease. And, to make cleaning a breeze, one side of the box should be removable.

A nest box isn't mandatory for a house bunny who lives in a quiet house. Instead many owners create a cozy area for their pets with loose bedding or a soft blanket. These are, of course, best used in a cage with solid flooring.

If you train your rabbit to use a litter box, you don't need a wire cage floor.

Where should you place your indoor rabbit's cage? Anywhere in the house that's relatively quiet, away from household traffic (but not too isolated), and draft-free. Rabbits are sensitive to cold drafts. Do not place an indoor cage near a window or outside door, and try not to place it directly on the floor during cold winter months. The cage should not be placed in a basement or other potentially damp area.

In addition, remember that rabbits are especially sensitive to heat. Do not place an indoor cage in direct sunshine or near a heat source such as a woodstove or fireplace. Rabbits cannot tolerate such extreme heat.

Outdoor Housing

For keeping rabbits outdoors, the traditional hutch, usually made of wood and wire (though many are made completely of metal), is a common choice. Ready-made hutches are fairly easy to find at pet or farm supply stores. Many rabbit enthusiasts swear by wood-and-wire hutches, noting that wooden hutches stay cool in the summer and warm in the winter. The primary disadvantages to wood are that rabbits chew it, and it is difficult to clean.

All-metal hutches have a devoted following among rabbit owners and breeders. Metal hutches are durable and easy to clean, and some are stackable. Metal, however, has a tendency to retain heat during hot weather and to be cold during winter months.

An outdoor hutch plays the important role of guardian and safekeeper to your rabbit when you're not there. Whatever type of hutch you buy, a wood-and-wire hutch or an all-metal hutch, make sure it's safe, secure, well constructed, and weather tight. It should have a roof, preferably pitched to shed rain, and it should be several feet off the ground. An outdoor hutch should have

Wood and wire are popular materials for outdoor hutches.

a wire bottom that allows the rabbit's droppings and urine to pass through. The floor wire shouldn't be large enough to allow the rabbit to snag a foot (no larger than 1 inch by 1 ½ inches). Avoid hutches made with chicken wire. Wire mesh is stronger than chicken wire and provides better defense against predators.

You want your outdoor rabbit to be comfortable, so a hutch should be roomy enough to allow her space to move about freely. A rabbit kept in a too-small enclosure can become overweight and depressed. Rabbit experts recommend providing a minimum of 1 square foot of space for each pound of rabbit. For example, the 4-pound Holland lop requires at least 4 square feet of space. Of course, you can always provide more.

Your outdoor hutch must protect your rabbit from the weather. You should have a way to batten down the hutch during rainy or windy weather (solid side panels or canvas drapes) or be able to block sunlight (a garden shade cloth works well). Protecting the cage sides is important because the elements don't always come straight from overhead. For example, while the roof might do a perfectly good job deflecting rain, the wire sides may welcome gusts of windy rain.

A nest box is essential to further protect the outdoor rabbit from cold or damp weather and to provide a sense of security (remember that in the wild, rabbits live in burrows). A nest box protects a rabbit from predators, such as cats and raccoons, who can reach through wire. You can fill the nest box with straw for extra warmth and comfort.

Where you place an outdoor rabbit hutch is another important consideration. Even though the hutch you purchase or build may be well made, consider placing it in a shed or outbuilding to further protect your rabbit against predators. Even the presence of a barking dog outside the cage can stress a rabbit severely.

Again, protect against weather extremes, too. Rabbits are especially sensitive to heat and high humidity; temperatures above 80° F can be dangerous. Place the hutch out of direct sunlight in an area that receives moderate sunlight and adequate shade. Rabbits are also sensitive to dampness and drafts. The hutch should be protected from drafts and high winds, though some ventilation is necessary.

Provide your outdoor rabbit with a nest box, which offers protection from weather and predators.

Indoor Safety

Just like any other pet, a rabbit is entirely dependent upon her caretakers. That means, once you bring Bunny home, you are responsible for feeding, nurturing, providing veterinary care, and grooming. You are responsible for your rabbit's safety. Your job is to provide the safest environment possible to minimize (hopefully eliminate) any chance of injury.

Just as parents of an active toddler must baby proof the home, rabbit owners who plan to keep their pet inside must rabbit proof. Rabbit proofing is essential! Rabbits are every bit as curious, inquisitive, and unaware of danger as a two-year-old child. If given free run (even supervised outings), rabbits are likely to get themselves into trouble: chewing electrical cords, eating books, or ingesting houseplants. You can prevent disaster, though, by rabbit proofing your home.

First, thwart the rabbit's propensity to chew everything in sight by removing tempting items. Cords of any kind are a big hit with rabbits: telephone, lamp, or stereo wires. Chewing on electrical wires is disastrous, so you must prevent it. The House Rabbit Society has some simple suggestions for making wires inaccessible to rabbits: decorative wire concealers, spiral cable wrap, and plastic PVC tubing.

The House Rabbit Society considers decorative wire concealers that stick to baseboards to be the most rabbit proof. This is the most costly and time-consuming method, though.

Spiral cable wrap can be purchased at an electronic store. Wrap electric and telephone cords in the spiral plastic sheath, which rabbits don't seem to want to chew. (Spiral cable wrap is flexible, so cords are still manageable.) Thin gauge, ½-inch

PVC tubing, which can be purchased at a hardware store, can also protect wires from your little chewer. Cut a slit in the tubes lengthwise with a sharp utility knife, and tuck the wires inside. This method also works with aquarium tubing.

Rabbits also chew wood items, which means furniture, baseboards, or knickknacks are likely targets. The best advice is to limit your rabbit's access to such items; you can cover furniture legs with plastic and move knickknacks out of your rabbit's reach. Offer your rabbit acceptable chewing toys instead.

A curious rabbit will graze, so beware houseplants! While houseplants may seem like a good snack, many are poisonous. Make sure all plants are inaccessible to the indoor rabbit. Hang plants if possible, but watch out for falling leaves. Better yet, eliminate houseplants altogether.

The curious rabbit is also a voracious chewer. Don't let your rabbit roam freely in rooms until you can remove or cover any wires within her reach.

Store other poisonous items such as household cleaners, laundry detergent, or furniture polish behind closed, locked doors. Invest in a few childproof latches for extra security.

Keep in mind that from the rabbit's point of view, anything on the floor is fair game. Don't leave anything lying around that you don't want investigated, nibbled, or shredded. Keep books (especially this one!), magazines, pens, pencils, shoes, plastic baby toys, and other important items away from your rabbit.

Cover electrical wires and phone cords in chew-proof tubing.

Top: Rabbit proofing before you let your rabbit have free reign of your home will protect both your plants and your rabbit from harm. Bottom: Secure cabinets containing chemicals with childproof (and rabbit-proof) latches.

Rabbit Supplies

In addition to housing, here are a few simple essentials you must purchase before bringing home a bunny. Most supplies can be purchased at pet or farm supply stores or through pet supply catalogs.

- Food bowls: Since rabbits can't resist chewing on or knocking over bowls, a heavy, ceramic crock made especially for small animals is in order. Make sure it's the right size for your rabbit breed, not too small or too large. Your rabbit should be able to reach in and eat comfortably.

- Water bottle: Clean, fresh water is essential to a rabbit's good health. But offering water in a bowl often means that it gets spilled (and then there's a wet rabbit and a big mess to clean up) or contaminated with food and droppings. Purchase a water bottle with a metal ball in the tip to regulate flow. Get the kind that hangs on the outside of the cage or hutch.

- Grooming tools: Daily brushing is necessary for wool breeds, so you'll need to purchase a soft slicker brush. Shorthair breeds can be groomed with a grooming mitt or with your hand.

- Hay rack: Many rabbit enthusiasts advocate feeding hay all the time but especially during molting. Hay adds roughage to a rabbit's diet, which aids digestion. Provide hay in a tiny hayrack that hangs on the cage or hutch. Keeping hay up off the cage floor helps keep the rabbit's living quarters cleaner.

- Litter box: Yes, rabbits can be trained to use a litter box, and if you're planning on keeping your bunny in the house, this is probably a wise goal. A litter box should fit both rabbit and cage—large enough to fit the rabbit but not so large that it dominates the enclosure.

- Litter: There are numerous opinions among rabbit enthusiasts regarding what litter is best. Natural/organic litters, those types made from wheat grass, aspen, or paper, are favorites. Avoid wood shavings made from cedar or pine, which are toxic to rabbits and other small animals.

- Bedding: Aspen wood shavings, straw, or a blanket are popular bedding choices. A small blanket works well for indoor cages; straw works for the outdoor hutch's nest box. Aromatic woods, such as pine and cedar, are considered by many experts to be dangerous to rabbits. Stay away from beddings made from these strong-smelling woods.

- Chew sticks: A rabbit's natural desire to chew must be considered. If you don't offer a safe, appropriate chew toy, your rabbit will find one of her own—which may not be so safe. Chewing sticks and blocks are available at pet supply stores.

- Toys: The playful rabbit enjoys toys. Specially made rabbit toys can be found at pet supply stores, but there's no reason you can't make a toy yourself. A paper plate or empty paper towel roll will keep a rabbit amused for hours.

- Harness and leash: You may want to teach Bunny to walk (hop) on a leash. If so, purchase a harness and leash made especially for rabbits; a cat harness and leash will work well too.

- Travel carrier: There may be occasions when you and Bunny must travel, such as to and from the vet's office. Travel safely by keeping Bunny in either a carrier made just for rabbits or a cat carrier.

Outdoor Safety

One of the greatest risks to rabbits kept in outdoor hutches is predators. Attacks usually occur at night, but they can also happen during the day. Even if you live in the city, you may still be visited by neighborhood cats, dogs, or wandering raccoons. Such visits can be deadly to pet rabbits, either if the predator is able to get into the hutch or if the rabbit panics, injures herself, and goes into shock due to the presence of a predator.

To prevent predators from harming your rabbit, make sure the hutch is secure. Latch doors securely. Instead of placing the hutch in a backyard where it's vulnerable to predators, place it in a shed. Consider bringing your rabbit in at night; confine her in a small cage or in a small, rabbit-proofed room.

Outdoor rabbits are in danger of being attacked by predators. Protect your pet with reliable fencing and your supervision.

Outdoor jaunts for house rabbits are fun, but they can be hazardous, too. Never allow your rabbit to run loose. Instead, teach her to walk on a leash or, better yet, use a daytime exercise pen. A child's ready-made play yard (playpen) works well for this. Supervise all playtimes. Never allow your rabbit to wander on grass that has been fertilized or sprayed with pesticides.

Family Introductions

Does your present household include dogs, cats, birds, or children? If so, before you bring a bunny home, you'll need to consider proper introductions. Since dogs and cats are predators, and birds and children can frighten the daylights out of rabbits, proper introductions are essential to building good relationships—and to create harmony in your home.

A rabbit's first few days in her new home can be nerve-racking, both for owner and rabbit. Your new rabbit is likely to feel nervous and anxious since she is unaccustomed to the strange surroundings. You are likely to feel a little nervous if this is your first pet rabbit, even though you've done your homework and are prepared. Try to relax. This is the beginning of a great friendship!

Introducing an indoor rabbit into the household is more complicated than bringing home a rabbit you plan to keep in an outdoor hutch. The former requires planning, the latter can be as simple as carrying the rabbit home and placing her in the prepared hutch.

Many households are already filled with other pets and people, including children. While these are all potential companions for the new rabbit, don't think friendships will develop in the first day, week, or even two weeks. Remembering that good relationships take time will make you all happier.

Introduce your rabbit to other household members slowly and gently. Taking time to do it properly will ensure good, long-lasting relationships.

When introducing a dog and a rabbit, keep them apart—preferably in separate rooms—but let them see each other.

Though they may seem to make unlikely companions, dogs and rabbits can become friends. Or at least live peaceably in the same house. The key to that, say dog trainers, is to be able to understand a dog's natural response to rabbits and be able to control it. That means, of course, working with an obedient dog, preferably an adult who listens and obeys commands. A dog's impulses toward a rabbit—mouthing and barking—aren't always predatory aggression, though they can be. Actions such as pawing or jumping around excitedly can merely be play behavior. While this behavior may mean play to the dog, it's a serious threat to a rabbit. Such antics scare rabbits—even scare them to death.

In the best case scenario, introducing an adult, obedience-trained dog and a rabbit would go like this: First, let the two species see each other, but don't put them in the same room. Keep the dog in one part of the house, the rabbit in the other. Let them become accustomed to each other's presence from a distance. Once the dog more or less ignores the rabbit in the other room, it's time to get a little closer. Put the dog on a lead and bring her into the rabbit's area. Don't allow the dog to lunge at the rabbit. If she does, correct her firmly. Do this until the dog ignores the bunny in the same room.

Rabbit experts suggest including the dog in daily bunny detail, such as cage cleaning, feeding, and the like. If your rabbit is at all disturbed by the dog's presence, though, promptly remove the dog. Eventually, with supervision, the dog will learn that rabbits aren't to be licked, pawed, attacked, or mouthed.

Cats and rabbits can become friends, too, though it's a relationship that must be cultivated. It is easier to introduce cats to medium- to large-size breeds. Cats are predators by nature— even friendly house cats hunt—so introductions must be taken slowly and with care. Keep the two separated at first (this may be a little more difficult to do than with a dog), and introduce them slowly. Always supervise interactions.

It's unlikely that the relationship between a pet bird and a rabbit will be close, but the two species can coexist. Take care not to allow your rabbit to be frightened by a bird's screeching or wing flapping. And don't allow your rabbit to charge a bird on the ground. Introduce the two slowly, and monitor all interactions closely.

Rabbits can also coexist with other small mammals such as guinea pigs. Introduce them slowly, perhaps by placing them together in the rabbit's exercise pen. Remove them immediately if one or the other becomes aggressive or frightened.

It may be more difficult to separate a rabbit and a cat. Never leave the two together unsupervised.

The First Day

Following are a few tips to make your rabbit's homecoming happy and stress-free.

- Have the hutch or cage set up with food bowls, toys, a water bottle, and a litter box.

- Rabbit proof the house.

- Designate a quiet area in which to confine the rabbit for the first few days.

- Read this book cover to cover.

- Brief all family members, especially children, on how to handle first interactions.

- Confine other pets.

- Ask the seller for a week's supply of the feed the rabbit has been eating.

- Cover the cage (of a new indoor rabbit) partially with a towel to provide security.

Introducing Rabbits to Other Rabbits

Rabbits can coexist with each other, too. But if you're a first-time owner, experts recommend keeping only one rabbit until you gain some experience and confidence in rabbit care. In time, you may want to acquire another rabbit.

This dog and rabbit have been properly introduced
and have developed a trusting bond.

Keeping two rabbits isn't as easy as it sounds, and introducing two rabbits can be more complicated than introducing a rabbit to the family dog or cat. By nature, rabbits are territorial, and in wild families there is a specific pecking order. When you introduce rabbits, their instincts tell them to determine their place in their social hierarchy. Rabbits who are strangers will undoubtedly act aggressively toward each other, and squabbles can result.

Intact rabbits are more likely to fight for pecking order, which is why many rabbit enthusiasts especially recommend spaying and neutering rabbits destined for multiple-rabbit homes. Minus the hormones and aggression that go along with being intact, altered rabbits are more likely to be calm and receptive to each other.

Gender can influence whether or not rabbits peaceably coexist. Spayed females and neutered males are most likely to become friends, but this isn't always the case. Neutered rabbits of both genders have been known to become best buddies with neutered members of their same sex.

An individual rabbit's temperament also has a role in friendships. Some rabbits are mellow and easygoing. Making friends with another rabbit isn't a big deal once initial introductions are done. Other rabbits are bossy with a "top bunny" mind-set.

Regardless of variables, all introductions must be gradual. Rabbits must work out a pecking order. Experts recommend introducing rabbits in neutral territory, where neither rabbit feels that he or she's on home turf. Keep the rabbits in their cages and simply place the cages several feet apart from each other in neither rabbit's territory (a spare bedroom, a car, or a friend's house). Work in twenty-minute sessions over a period of several days.

Next comes a face-to-face introduction. Let the rabbits meet outside their cages in neutral territory, with each rabbit fitted with a harness and leash. A harness allows you to separate the two should they start fighting. Allow the rabbits to go near each other, but don't let them get close enough to touch. Do this for several days.

Eventually you can allow them to get closer together (still in harness) in the neutral area. If (and probably when) a fight breaks out, the House Rabbit Society recommends spraying the rabbits with a quick squirt of water from a spray bottle. This won't hurt the rabbits, but it should startle them so they stop fighting. In time, the rabbits will learn to tolerate each other and may even become best friends.

Top right: When making introductions, you can maintain better control if the rabbits are fitted with a harness and leash. Bottom right: Make sure that introduction sessions are done in neither rabbit's territory.

Introducing Children and Rabbits

Children thoroughly enjoy rabbits, and rabbits can enjoy children, as well. It's important to remember, though, that rabbits are not good pets for children under seven years of age. These youngsters don't really have the skills to handle a rabbit properly. They can be taught, of course, but an adult must be carefully monitor interactions to ensure the rabbit's safety.

Don't let children pick up a new rabbit right away, and let the rabbit go to the children herself as she's ready.

Don't allow children to "rush" the rabbit on her first day at home. This is difficult because having a new pet is exciting to youngsters. It's best, however, to place the cage in a quiet area of the house, a rabbit-proofed bathroom or spare bedroom for example, and simply open the cage door. Avoid reaching in to pick up the rabbit, and don't allow children to do it either. Allow the rabbit to hop out on her own accord; she will—rabbits are curious. Have the child sit quietly and just watch. As time goes on and the rabbit seems more relaxed, the child may speak soothingly and pet the animal. A child younger than seven years should not pick up a rabbit since mishandling can result in breaking a rabbit's back.

Keep interactions quiet and low-key, and monitor the child and rabbit carefully. Give the rabbit time to explore and feel comfortable in her new environment. Bonding with family members, whether they are adults, children, dogs, or cats, takes time.

Healthful Food

A diet of nutritious food and plenty of fresh water is important to keeping a rabbit healthy. Rabbits are herbivores and need a well-balanced, fibrous diet of proteins, fats, vitamins, carbohydrates, and minerals. As an owner, you are responsible for providing your rabbit with food that meets her nutritional needs.

The best way to give your rabbit the correct balance of nutrients, according to many rabbit experts, is to feed commercial rabbit pellets along with daily vegetables. Pellets are formulated with the rabbit's specific nutritional needs in mind, so feeding a rabbit is not complicated. Simply fill the rabbit's crock with pellets and let the eating begin. Which pellets should you buy? Ask the breeder or your veterinarian for a suggestion. Rabbit experts recommend any brand that contains 18 to 20 percent crude fiber and 16 to 20 percent protein. A diet should also contain phos-phorus, calcium, and vitamins. Before buying, read the labeling to check percentages and ingredients.

Be sure the pellets are fresh. Check the manufacturing date before purchasing. Moldy feed is toxic to rabbits. When you open the sack of pellets, take a whiff. It should smell like a bale of fresh alfalfa hay. If it doesn't smell or smells bad, return it.

But pellets seem so boring, you say? Doesn't a rabbit need some carrots to nibble? Some rabbit experts say that a diet of qua-li-ty pellets and water is sufficient; however, many rabbit enthu-siasts and veterinarians recommend feeding roots and dark-green vegetables every day. To avoid diarrhea associated with changes in diet and with high-moisture foods such as fruits and vegeta-bles, start out feeding your rabbit tiny amounts of these foods (no iceberg lettuce, though) and gradually increase the amount. Fresh vegetables shouldn't be given in large amounts. The House

Fresh pellets smell like alfalfa hay.

Many rabbit experts recommend feeding rabbits fresh vegetables.

Rabbit Society suggests 1 cup of vegetables for every 4 pounds of body weight, but check with your veterinarian for the right amount for your rabbit.

Don't offer sweets to your rabbit. While rabbits love the taste of sweet foods, they cannot tolerate sugars or carbohydrates. Too much sugar can contribute to an overgrowth of the wrong kind of bacteria in a rabbit's digestive system. Under no circum-stances should rabbits younger than six months old be offered greens, carrots, cabbage, lettuce, or other fresh veggies. Eating those foods may kill them.

Even though pellets already contain some fiber, keep hay available at all times to add roughage to the diet. Small bales of alfalfa and timothy hay are available at pet supply stores.

Pellets, greens, and some hay: that's about all the food you need to purchase before bringing home a bunny. Isn't simplicity wonderful?

CHAPTER FIVE

The Best of Care

Do you want to be the best rabbit owner in the world? Then learn as much as you can about how to take care of your new rabbit! Following is care information that will help keep your rabbit healthy and enhance your relationship.

Feeding

Most rabbit experts recommend commercial pellets as the staple of the rabbit's diet. But given the rabbit's tender digestive nature, there's a lot more to feeding rabbits that new owners must understand.

Probably the most important aspect of feeding rabbits is consistency. Rabbits cannot tolerate drastic changes in diet. Experts who advocate a pellet-only diet for rabbits do so because pellets provide consistency. Pellets are formulated to provide all the nutrients essential to a rabbit's good health, and they do so without digestive upset. Many rabbit experts believe that the pellets alone don't provide enough fiber, though, so always keep a hayrack with fresh hay available for your rabbit.

A domestic rabbit is dependent upon his owner for food. You are, essentially, the rabbit's waiter for life. That means you are responsible for serving your new friend every day. If you're going to be away for the weekend or gone past your rabbit's suppertime, you must arrange for a friend or family member to feed your pet. Always remember that a rabbit cannot hop to the feed bag and help himself.

Depending on who you talk to—vets, breeders, enthusiasts, authors—you will encounter varying opinions regarding diet. As mentioned, some rabbit experts advocate a diet of pellets only. But many other experts and vets believe a rabbit's diet must be supplemented with fresh vegetables, especially greens and roots. The best advice is to follow the feeding recommendations of a veterinarian who is knowledgeable about rabbits. If your rabbit thrives, doesn't suffer diarrhea, looks healthy, and is a healthy weight for his breed, you can assume the diet is appropriate.

Many owners wish to give their rabbits treats in addition to a regular diet. While treats aren't necessary, they are fun. As long as a rabbit is receiving a proper diet, there's no harm in an occasional treat. Common treats include apples, carrots, oatmeal, alfalfa cubes, greens, and roots. Feed treats in small amounts—a slice of apple, a melon cube, or a small handful of oatmeal—after the rabbit has eaten his regular diet. Do not feed your rabbit sugary foods, and avoid commercially prepared treats that contain sugar, salt, or chocolate.

Feeding Guidelines

There are a lot of fat bunnies these days, according to veterinarians. Some experts attribute this to people overfeeding pellets to rabbits and to lack of exercise. Obesity is unhealthy for rabbits, just as it is for people. Don't overfeed your rabbit, and make sure he gets plenty of activity to burn calories. How much should you feed your rabbit? Well, that can be difficult to determine, and it depends upon what you're feeding him. A rabbit expert offers advice. Generally:

- Free-feed (keep the food bowl filled) young, growing rabbits. Leave a bowl of pellets in the cage at all times.

- Do not free-feed adults or rabbits older than six to eight months.

- Gradually cut back the quantity of feed available to young rabbits.

- Giant breeds, those that weigh 12 to 20 pounds at maturity, usually consume 6 ounces of pellets daily; breeds that weigh 8 to 12 pounds at maturity, 4 ounces a day; breeds that weigh 4 to 8 pounds, 2 ounces a day; and dwarf breeds (those that weigh less than 4 pounds) require 1 ounce a day.

- If your rabbit doesn't eat all the pellets in his bowl, you may be feeding too much.

- Split feedings. Feed half the ration in the morning and half in the evening.

- Feed at the same time(s) every day.

- In addition to a proper diet, a rabbit needs water. Make sure your rabbit has easy access to clean, fresh water at all times.

Rabbits also enjoy nibbling on twigs or branches. Dried and aged fruit tree branches (apple tree is a favorite) are a wonderful treat. Be sure to offer only twigs that have not been sprayed with pesticides, and offer only dried and aged twigs. Some tree branches, such as branches from cherry, peach, apricot, plum, and redwood trees, are poisonous to rabbits, as are many fresh branches. Dried apple tree branches are safe for rabbits. Ask an experienced rabbit vet or a local House Rabbit Society volunteer in your area for the best place to find aged, rabbit-safe branches.

Grooming

When it comes to grooming rabbits, there really is not a lot of work involved. Most breeds get by with simple petting or stroking with a grooming mitt to remove hair. The only exception to this is the wool breeds, which require brushing at least three to four times a week, but every day is best.

The naturally clean rabbit continuously licks himself and ingests hair, especially during molting (shedding) periods. This can result in hair balls. Prevent hair balls by feeding a high-fiber diet and simply stroking the rabbit with your hand, head to tail, once a week. Lightly dampen (not wet) your hands with water and pet with the lay of fur until all the excess hair is removed. Not only does this simple act of petting remove hair, but it also

Did You Know?

One Angora rabbit provides enough wool each year to make one short-sleeved sweater.

Gently pet your bunny with a grooming mitt to remove excess hair.

helps distribute natural oils. And it's pleasurable for both you and your bunny! You can also use a grooming mitt or soft bristle slicker. Brushing can be irritating to a rabbit's sensitive skin, however, so keep brushing to a minimum. If you do brush your rabbit, do it gently. Wool breeds are a labor of love. Plan on brushing a rabbit who is a wool breed with a soft slicker brush at least three times a week or every day if needed.

Grooming time is an excellent opportunity to check your rabbit for signs of illness. As you pet or brush him, look for hints of diarrhea, runny eyes or nose, or sores. Check the ears for signs of ear mites. Check for fleas, too. Just like dogs and cats, rabbits are subject to the misery of these biting bugs. If you see fleas or flea dirt (dark brown specks), try combing them out with a flea comb. Or give your vet a call. He or she can recommend flea control products that are safe for rabbits. Avoid bathing your rabbit unless the infestation is severe and a vet advises it.

Though you'll find plenty of rabbit shampoos on the market, full-body bathing isn't a good idea. Most rabbit experts advise against bathing rabbits because bathing stresses them too severely. Rabbits don't need baths and are susceptible to chilling afterward. The best way to keep your rabbit clean is by housing him in a clean environment. Spot clean your rabbit now and then if needed.

Regular nail trimming is important for both you and your rabbit. Regular trims prevent painful nail tears (should the rabbit catch a nail on cage wire), and trimming prevents you from being scratched with long, sharp nails when you handle your pet. Check the nails every week, but trimming is usually necessary only once a month or so. Either clippers made for cats or a pair of human clippers is sufficient.

Left: As part of your grooming routine, check your rabbit's ears for ear mites. Above: Rabbits need their nails trimmed every six to eight weeks.

Trimming nails isn't difficult, but many owners are wary of the chore because they're afraid of cutting a nail too short and making it bleed. The trick is to clip off just the tips. That's usually all that's necessary, anyway. Hold your rabbit securely and clip with short, decisive strokes. Avoid the quick (a pinkish vein in the nail). If you cut too much, apply a pinch of styptic powder to stop the bleeding.

Handling

How to pick up or hold a rabbit is a little intimidating to new owners. And it's okay to be somewhat apprehensive. There are right ways and wrong ways to handle rabbits. You want to do what's best and safest for you and your bunny. Rabbit experts advise owners to wear long-sleeved shirts. Rabbits have sharp claws and a scratch on a bare arm is painful. Also, a rabbit might have an accident—urinate or defecate—while being handled. (Rabbit-show judges sometimes wear special jackets or smocks to protect their clothing.) So choose a shirt you don't care might be ruined. The goal in handling your rabbit is to pick him up and hold him in a way that makes him feel secure and comfortable. Otherwise, he may scratch, kick, or struggle. Holding a rabbit should be a good experience for you both.

The best way to lift and carry a small rabbit is to grasp the rabbit by the loose skin right above the shoulders. Then slide your other hand under the rabbit's body to support the hindquarters. Gently lift the rabbit and bring him toward your body and hold him firmly and securely. Larger rabbits should not be lifted by the scruff but rather with one hand under the chest and the other hand supporting the rump. Always lift your rabbit out of

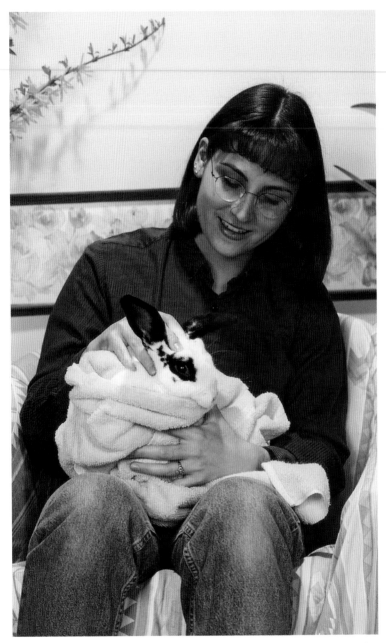

If your rabbit has a tendency to kick or scratch when handled, wear long sleeves and wrap the rabbit in a towel when you hold him.

his cage head first, and take care not to let his legs drag against the cage's wire floor to avoid catching a toenail. Return your rabbit to his cage tail-first.

Never pick up your rabbit by his ears, and don't grab him by the legs. Not only does this scare the animal but it's harmful.

Pick up a rabbit by first grasping the loose skin on the back of the neck and supporting the rabbit's weight from underneath.

Rabbits need to become accustomed to being handled, so expect some struggles at first. In time, rabbits accept and enjoy handling, although they are individuals and some enjoy being held more than others. Be sensitive to that. Always be gentle and make handling a regular practice.

Be sure your rabbit feels secure while you're holding him.

Cleanup

Cleanup detail is an essential, though mundane, part of keeping rabbits. Whether your rabbit lives in the house with you or in an outdoor hutch, you must keep his quarters clean.

Keeping a rabbit indoors means cleaning the litter box as needed, usually twice a week for one rabbit. Empty the litter, rinse the pan with hot water, then add a splash of vinegar or an enzymatic cleaner to eliminate the rabbit's strong urine odor. Rinse with plain water, then dry completely before adding clean litter. Check the rabbit's cage daily to see if it needs cleaning, too. Remove dirty bedding right away and check the nest box to see if it needs cleaning. Wash the cage and nest box once a week (or as needed) with a solution of one part bleach to four parts water.

Control odors and keep your rabbit healthy by cleaning his cage before you notice any odor.

Outdoor cages need to be cleaned regularly as well.

Rinse well. Be sure to let the cage dry completely before allowing the rabbit to have access to it. Wash food and water dishes or bottles daily.

Around the house, clean up urine and fecal matter with soap and water. You may need to treat carpets or other surfaces specifically as directed by the product's manufacturer.

Though some say an outdoor hutch is "self-cleaning," don't believe it. You must clean an outdoor rabbit's quarters just as you must clean an indoor cage and litter box. Scrape off fecal matter, and scrub the wires with the diluted bleach solution. Rinse the wires and let them dry before placing the rabbit back in the hutch.

Training

A great way to spend time with your pet rabbit is to take on the challenge of teaching him a few lessons, for example litter box training or walking on a leash. Rabbits are excellent students, and most are fairly easy to train. According to the House Rabbit Society, training will be easier for you if you understand that a rabbit's behavior is usually motivated by one of three things: a natural inclination to chew and dig, a need to communicate, and social structure. This means that when you're trying to teach your rabbit not to chew electrical cords in the house for instance, you must understand that his desire to chew is natural. No amount of training can change that, nor should your goal in training be to stop the rabbit from chewing. Your goal is to teach the rabbit to chew safe items provided by you.

Another factor to keep in mind is that training young rabbits, like training puppies and kittens, is more challenging than teaching adults. Kits are full of energy and have a need to explore: settling down for lessons is tough. Be especially patient with youngsters, and don't set expectations too high. Learning new skills requires time and effort. Be willing to spend time every day teaching your bunny. The more you put into it, the greater the results—and rewards!

Remember to start small. Rabbits learn best if trained within a small area. As a bunny becomes trustworthy in one room, such as a laundry room, you can increase the boundaries gradually. Most important, be consistent and offer plenty of praise. Avoid scolding Bunny. Rabbits are sensitive, and scolding only confuses and frightens them.

Above: Place your rabbit in the litter box several times a day to train him to use it.
Below: After the rabbit learns to use the box, teach your rabbit to return to the cage to use the litter box. Keep the training area small.

One of the first things you may want to teach your rabbit is how to use a litter box. The rabbit's propensity toward cleanliness—in the wild a rabbit doesn't foul his or her own den—makes him receptive to the idea. It's natural for a rabbit to pick one spot to do business in and return there consistently when nature calls. All an owner needs to do is figure out which spot and furnish it with a litter box. What kind of litter box? Pick one to fit the rabbit. You don't want it too big or too small. Check a few pet supply stores for litter boxes; either those made for cats or those made especially for rabbits work best. Organic paper fillers are best because dusty clay- and wood-based litters can cause respiratory problems. Place the litter box in the area of the cage where the

As you slowly increase your rabbit's roaming area, add an extra litter box or two for insurance.

rabbit normally relieves himself, and put a few fecal pellets in the box to give him the right idea. To encourage the rabbit to hop in, you can place a small amount of hay in the box as well. With any luck, your rabbit will take the hint and use the box.

The next step in litter box training is to teach your rabbit to return to the cage after a supervised outing. It's best to begin this process with the cage in a small, rabbit-proofed room such as a bathroom. Remember that you'll be most successful if you train your rabbit in one small area at a time. Watch your rabbit closely when you take him out to play. If he starts to urinate, promptly place him in the litter box. The idea is to get the rabbit to associate toilet activities with the litter box.

Some rabbits enjoy sitting in the litter box, munching on the hay you have placed there. Other rabbits may take a nap, but hanging out in the litter box for long periods isn't healthy. Damp litter contains fungal and bacterial growth. Provide your rabbit an alternative resting place with soft bedding, and clean the box frequently.

Once your rabbit gets the idea of returning to the litter box (to go to the bathroom) in a small area, you can expand the boundaries. Increase the size of the area a little at time, say, moving from the bathroom only to the bathroom and a hallway. Keep the litter box in the cage and place one or two other litter boxes in the new area. Hopefully, the idea of the litter box is firmly planted in the rabbit's mind and he will choose to use the extras if nature calls. Don't make the mistake of increasing the area too quickly, though, or you'll be cleaning up a mess.

Litter training takes time, but it's really worth your patience. A litter-trained rabbit can hop freely about your home (supervised, of course), and you don't have to worry about carpet or flooring stains and smells.

Not only can a rabbit learn to use a litter box but he also can learn to walk on a leash. It's quite a sight to see a leash-trained rabbit hopping alongside his owner. Though it may be unusual, it's extremely practical. Teaching your rabbit to accept a harness and leash offers extra safety that comes in handy, say, when taking your rabbit to the vet.

Begin by purchasing a harness and leash at a pet supply store. You can buy a set made especially for rabbits, but one made for cats works well, too. Simply buckle on the harness and let the rabbit hop around. (Don't use a neck collar, which can be dangerous.) Watch him closely. Once the rabbit becomes accustomed to the harness (this may take a few days), snap on the leash. Walk around the house. Keep in mind that walking a rabbit is better described as the rabbit walking you. The rabbit hops and you follow. Rabbits cannot be trained to walk on a leash in the same way dogs can be trained, so don't expect Bunny to heel. Having your rabbit on-lead, however, does give him a little freedom while providing you some control.

Stay indoors until your rabbit is completely comfortable with the leash and harness. Then venture outdoors, say in a fenced yard or other safe environment. It's especially important to be on the lookout for potential dangers—a barking dog for example—while outside. Rabbits are easily frightened and stressed. Be careful when walking your rabbit outdoors—a loose dog can quickly injure or kill a rabbit. The goal of a walk is to have fun, not end in disaster.

Top left: Let your rabbit get used to wearing a harness for a few days before attaching a leash. Bottom left: A rabbit enjoys going for a hop around the house for some exercise once he grows accustomed to a harness and leash.

Travel

It seems wonderful: taking Bunny along everywhere you go, traveling here and there with a lagomorph friend in tow. Hop in the car for a country drive, catch a plane to Europe, board a train going west. Indeed, travels with Bunny is a great fantasy!

The reality is that rabbits are timid creatures prone to stress in new situations. Stress causes a rabbit to become susceptible to illness. A stressed rabbit soon becomes a sick rabbit. For the most part, traveling with Bunny is not a good idea—and experts don't recommend it. If you're planning a vacation, it's best to hire a pet-sitter.

Travel Tips

There are times when it's necessary to transport your bunny, such as a trip to the vet or when moving to a new home. If you must transport your rabbit, you must do it safely and without stressing the animal. Following are a few tips to help you do just that:

- For added safety, buy a travel hutch that attaches to a seat belt. For more added security, fill the travel hutch with hay or place a towel on the cage bottom.

- Avoid transporting a rabbit by airplane. Not all airlines permit animals on board, and if they do, the animal must be in a cage that fits under the seat. That means large rabbits are sent to the cargo area where temperatures are not usually regulated.

- Purchase a travel hutch or rabbit carrier commonly used by breeders to transport rabbits to and from shows. A cat carrier will also do.

- Plan ahead and be prepared if you're moving. Check state and city pet ordinances where you're going, and if you'll be renting, make sure the landlord allows pets.

- Never leave a rabbit in an enclosed vehicle, and don't travel by car when temperatures are extremely high.

- Keep the travel cage out of direct sunlight and away from cold drafts.

- Do not tranquilize your rabbit unless directed to do so by a veterinarian. If your vet recommends medicating your rabbit, administer a dose prior to traveling to see how the rabbit responds to the medication. A pet's reactions to a sedative can be difficult to predict. If your pet has a bad reaction to the tranquilizer, do not administer it for the trip.

CHAPTER SIX

To Health!

GOOD HEALTH IS A BLESSING. IT'S ALSO THE RESULT OF a simple but little-used practice: preventive care. You know, providing care *before* a health problem arises. The best way to ensure that a new pet rabbit stays bright eyed and healthy once you bring her home is to practice preventive care. Following that, you must be on the lookout for signs of illness, which aren't always easy to detect in rabbits. Before a problem arises, you must locate a vet who treats rabbits. Being familiar with the common diseases that affect rabbits is helpful, too.

Preventive Care

Feed your rabbit a nutritious diet that meets her particular needs, and you're likely to have a healthy rabbit. We are what we eat, and the same applies to rabbits. If your rabbit doesn't receive the proper nutrients, she is more prone to illness. Ask your veterinarian to recommend a high-quality commercial pellet diet, and feed the right amount for your rabbit's weight. Offer plenty of fresh water and hay. Be sure to store the food properly to preserve vitamins and prevent spoilage, and use only fresh pellets.

Cleanliness is next to godliness, or at least it's a surefire way to prevent illness. Rabbits need clean, dry housing to keep healthy. Use highly absorbent bedding, and remove wet bedding right away. Humidity and dampness make rabbits susceptible to respiratory infections. Daily cleaning of the cage or hutch, water bottle, crock, and other cage accessories can prevent potential illness while preventing unpleasant odors, too. Remember, rabbits don't have a body odor; they're naturally clean animals. But rabbit urine has a strong ammonia odor that's unpleasant to both rabbits and owners.

Rabbits also need appropriate housing to remain healthy. Take care to select a hutch or cage to meet your particular rabbit's needs. A hutch or cage must be safe, the right size, and comfortable. Ill-suited housing can stress a rabbit, which can make her more prone to illness. It's best to house unneutered adult rabbits separately, too. Intact males and females will mate. Mature males have a tendency to fight, as do intact females, although with great time and care, some house rabbits (especially if neutered) can be taught to accept other rabbits.

It's okay to hold and hug your bunny, but be sure to handle her carefully. Proper handling is essential to the rabbit's safety and yours. Rabbits have strong back legs with claws. If handled improperly, a nervous bunny could scratch you, which could cause you to let go. Rabbits are fairly delicate, and a fall could

Support your rabbit's weight and hug her close to your body so that if she struggles, you won't drop her.

result in a broken back. Take time to learn how to lift and carry your bunny, and be sure to teach other family members, especially youngsters, the same to prevent accidents.

Unlike some high-maintenance pets who require hours of primping to look good (poodles, for example), rabbits don't need a lot of grooming to look good and stay healthy. Like cats, rabbits clean themselves. But they do require some additional grooming by their owners, usually brushing, nail trimming, and ear checks. Rabbits stay clean and healthy with simple petting and brushing, and most importantly, by being kept in a clean cage or hutch.

Veterinarians experienced in rabbit care recommend spaying or neutering pet rabbits. Not only does this prevent unwanted litters but also your altered rabbit will be a healthier, better-adjusted pet. Altered rabbits are less prone to aggression, urine spraying, and other undesirable sexual behaviors. Quite simply, altered rabbits make better pets.

Besides keeping your rabbit healthy, neutering will prevent unwanted litters.

Spaying and neutering prevent certain health problems, too. Research shows that as much as 80 percent of certain populations of unspayed female rabbits over the age of two years have uterine cancer. Uterine cancer is the leading cause of death in females over two years old. While this doesn't mean that all does will be affected, it indicates a high risk factor. Spaying, especially between the ages of four and six months, eliminates the risk.

An excellent way to prevent complications from elective surgeries such as spaying and neutering is to make sure the rabbit is in good health prior to the procedure. A healthy bunny is best able to recover and heal from surgery. Some vets recommend a presurgical exam, which may include blood tests to detect potential problems.

Rabbit vets usually do not recommend withholding food prior to a bunny's surgery. Drastic changes in diet and feeding can upset a rabbit's sensitive digestive tract and could result in postoperative complications. Ask your vet for precise presurgical instructions.

Proper care after surgery is essential, too. Some hospitals keep rabbits overnight; others send them home later in the day. When you pick up your rabbit, be sure to ask for specific home-care instructions. Most likely, the vet will recommend confining your rabbit in an indoor cage for a few days (two days for males, five or six days for females). Keep a close watch on your rabbit for signs of infection. Your rabbit should be at least nibbling on food the day after surgery and eating normally in two days. Call your vet right away if you have any questions or concerns.

Just as regular exercise is good for you, it's good for Bunny, too. Don't allow your rabbit to overeat, and make sure she gets plenty of playtime. If you don't, you're likely to have a fat rabbit on your hands—and that's unhealthy. Prevent obesity with daily exercise: outings in an exercise pen, walks on the leash, or romps through the living room.

Remember the discussion on safety? You can prevent tragedy by simply rabbit proofing your home or hutch. Always supervise your pet, especially during interactions with other pets or children. It is always better to be safe than sorry!

Continue to feed your rabbit her regular meals before surgery unless your vet recommends otherwise.

Last, but not least of preventive care suggestions, it's a good idea to get connected with an experienced rabbit practitioner before an emergency arises. Though rabbits are usually healthy if kept properly, you never know when problems can arise. Not all veterinarians are well versed in the latest rabbit care. In case of illness, you want a doctor who is.

Being overweight is not healthy for a rabbit. Monitor your rabbit's food intake and encourage regular exercise.

Finding a
Rabbit Veterinarian

Getting connected with an experienced rabbit practitioner is easier said than done. One reason is that there just isn't a large number of vets specially trained in rabbit medicine. Veterinary students interested in treating rabbits and other small mammals are limited by school curriculums; they usually learn about rabbits through internships with experienced practitioners. Be that as it may, it is possible to locate vets who understand and treat rabbits.

Ask other rabbit owners or breeders for a referral. Word of mouth from experienced rabbit enthusiasts is usually the best way to learn about an experienced rabbit vet. You can also contact a local House Rabbit Society volunteer. House Rabbit Society volunteers are usually delighted to assist new rabbit owners in learning about rabbit care, including helping them find a vet.

You can go on-line to find a rabbit vet. Search the Internet for rabbit forums, rabbit enthusiasts, and rabbit vets. Or check your local yellow pages for veterinarians who list rabbits or other exotics in their ads. Call several vets in your area and ask who treats rabbits. Once you locate a vet who treats rabbits, ask him or her which rabbit medicine conferences he or she has attended recently. You want to choose a vet who is up to date on the latest treatments.

Though rabbits do not require routine vaccinations as do other domestic pets, such as dogs and cats, a yearly checkup is a good idea. And, as previously mentioned, spaying and neutering are recommended, too.

Find a vet who specializes in treating rabbits and other small animals.

Typical Health Concerns

In spite of an owner's vigilance, there are times when a rabbit becomes ill. How will you know if your rabbit's sick? Well, a rabbit can't tell you when she feels lousy, so you must learn to observe your pet and read the signs of illness. Take note of any sudden change in your rabbit's behavior or physical condition. If you notice a problem, give your vet a call.

There are countless bacterial diseases, viral diseases, parasitic conditions, and noninfectious ailments that can affect domestic rabbits. Fortunately, most pet rabbits live healthy lives as long as they're well kept. But just in case, here are a few common conditions that affect pet rabbits.

The most common health problems in rabbits involve the gastrointestinal tract and for good reason: the rabbit has a specialized and sensitive digestive system. A sudden change in diet can result in diarrhea. The telltale signs of diarrhea are dirty hindquarters—a healthy rabbit is clean—and loose or runny droppings. A healthy rabbit's dropping are hard and well formed. While an abrupt change in diet could be the cause, diarrhea could also signal a serious illness that requires immediate treatment. Don't delay. Contact your veterinarian at the first signs of diarrhea.

There's a price rabbits pay for keeping clean. The naturally neat rabbit ingests quite a bit of hair while licking and grooming herself. Since rabbits cannot vomit, what goes in must come out the other end. Unfortunately, hair doesn't always come out, especially if the rabbit isn't getting enough roughage in her diet. A rabbit with a hair blockage can have periodic diarrhea, hair in the stool, loss of appetite, or weight loss. Consult with your veterinarian if you suspect a hair blockage.

Rabbits swallow a lot of hair when they groom themselves. Breeds with longer hair, such as this fuzzy lop, may be at a higher risk for hair blockages.

Regular brushing, especially during the shedding season, is one of the best ways to prevent hair balls. In addition, your vet may recommend additional treatments such as increasing fiber in the diet and/or administering a hair ball remedy.

While you may love soaking up sunshine and temperatures above 80° F, rabbits have little tolerance for hot weather; they're susceptible to heatstroke. High temperatures accompanied by high humidity are the worst culprits. Signs of heatstroke may include lethargy, rapid breathing, a wet nose and mouth, and your rabbit may sprawl on the cage floor. If your rabbit shows these signs, consider it an emergency. Quickly move Bunny to a cooler spot, and place her up to her neck in cool water or under damp towels. Call your vet right away.

To prevent heatstroke, always be aware of your rabbit's environment. Outdoor cages should be placed in the shade.

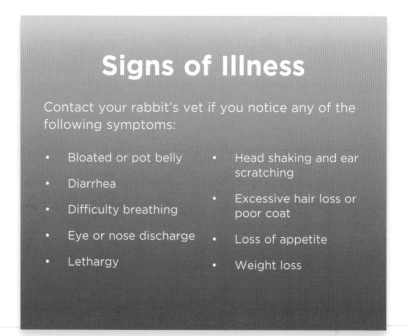

Signs of Illness

Contact your rabbit's vet if you notice any of the following symptoms:

- Bloated or pot belly
- Diarrhea
- Difficulty breathing
- Eye or nose discharge
- Lethargy

- Head shaking and ear scratching
- Excessive hair loss or poor coat
- Loss of appetite
- Weight loss

Run fans and the air conditioner during hot weather to prevent heatstroke.

In preparation for especially hot weather, fill large plastic bottles (a 2-liter soda bottle or a 1-gallon milk container) with water and freeze them. (It's a good idea to keep a bottle of water in the freezer during warm months so that you always have one when you need it.) Place the frozen jug in the hutch so the rabbit can lie against it to keep cool. Keep tabs on the temperatures indoors, too. Run the air conditioner and fans during hot weather.

Rabbits can suffer from a condition called malocclusion in which their teeth do not properly meet. A rabbit's ever-growing teeth must meet evenly in order to wear down properly, otherwise they just keep growing! The results of uneven wear are not only long teeth but also eating difficulties, mouth sores, and jaw problems. If left on her own, a rabbit suffering "buck" or "wolf" teeth will starve because she can't eat. The story doesn't have to end sadly, though. Regular teeth trimming by a veterinarian can turn things around.

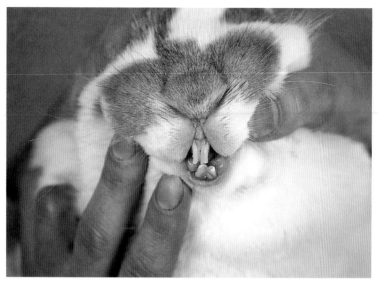

Malocclusion is a serious condition in which a rabbit's teeth don't meet evenly.

The signs of pasteurellosis, a bacterial upper respiratory infection commonly called "snuffles," are persistent sneezing, nasal discharge, and coughing. A rabbit suffering from snuffles is a sick rabbit indeed. Pneumonia is frequently a secondary complication. This highly contagious ailment can be transmitted in air and on hands and must be treated by a veterinarian. Pasteurellosis can be fatal.

Another deadly disease afflicting rabbits is myxomatosis. In fact, the disease is credited with killing off large numbers of wild rabbits throughout Europe in the 1800s. Myxomatosis is still deadly today and is seen primarily in coastal areas of California and Oregon during May through August. The disease causes severe conjunctivitis, high fever, and respiratory infection. It is transmitted by mosquitoes and biting flies. Take your rabbit to the vet if you notice these symptoms.

While wire cage bottoms make cleanup easy for owners, wire floors can take a toll on a rabbit's feet. Rabbits can develop a condition known as sore hocks—red, swollen skin accompanied by hair loss—from constant contact with a wire floor. A vet may prescribe an antibiotic ointment to promote healing. Providing your rabbit with alternative (solid) flooring helps prevent sore hocks. Some owners place a small board or two in the hutch bottom (away from where the rabbit usually eliminates). This enables the rabbit to hop off the wire occasionally, preventing sore feet.

The best way to prevent a wet dewlap (a pendulous fold of skin beneath the chin) is to provide a water bottle. A wet dewlap results from constantly being dragged in a water bowl. The wet fur becomes matted and a secondary bacterial infection often results. The condition must be treated by a veterinarian, who may clip the fur and prescribe antibiotic ointment.

The signs of urinary stones, or calciuria, are poor appetite, frequent or painful urination, and passing sandlike stones. A rabbit suffering from calciuria may be reluctant to move and may sit in a hunched-up posture due to a painful bladder. The rabbit may pass small calculi, commonly called sand or sludge, in the urine. The exact cause of calciuria is poorly defined, but some researchers believe it's linked to a diet high in calcium. It may also be caused by neurological problems such as back trauma or congenital abnormalities that make it difficult for rabbits to empty their bladder. The condition must be treated by a veterinarian.

Rabbits are affected by both internal and external parasites. Coccidia are microscopic parasites that affect the intestinal tract and liver of rabbits and other animals. Signs of infestation (coccidiosis) include weight loss, poor appetite, diarrhea, or bloated abdomen. A veterinarian must treat coccidiosis; it can be fatal. Prevention depends upon keeping rabbits in a clean environment and having new pet rabbits, especially those with unfamiliar backgrounds (such as shelter bunnies), quarantined for thirty days before introducing them to a rabbitry or a household with rabbits.

Ear mites, which commonly affect cats and dogs, can also trouble rabbits. Head shaking and ear scratching are common signs. You may also see a dark brown, waxy substance in the ear canal. If you see this, consult with your vet. Ear mites are an annoying problem that requires medication to eradicate. Fur mites, another type of mite, are little buggers that result in hair loss and red, scabby patches. They, too, must be treated by a vet.

Ear mite infestations are irritating.

Comb your rabbit regularly with a fine-toothed flea comb to keep your pet flea-free.

Rabbits can also suffer from a mange mite infestation. Intense itching, resulting in a lot of scratching, is a common symptom. There's also a loss of hair on the chin, head, ears, and neck. A visit to the vet is in order to curb this problem.

Fleas, the same biting critters that attack dogs and cats, can attack rabbits, too. Fortunately, rabbits are not commonly affected, as long as other household pets are flea-free. The tell-tale sign of the buggers is "flea dirt," brown-black flecks that look like dirt, or you may even see fleas hopping about. Fleas must be eradicated, and the best way to do so—with the least stress to the rabbit—is to use a flea comb. If your rabbit is heavily infested, ask your veterinarian to recommend a rabbit-safe flea powder or spray. Avoid bathing your rabbit, which is terribly stressful for rabbits (the dampness isn't good either).

Rabbits are excellent pets, but sometimes being a pet can be stressful for a rabbit given the species' naturally timid temperament. Loud noise, household traffic, frequent handling, or temperature changes can take a toll on Bunny, causing her to be susceptible to illness. To prevent stress, avoid frightening your rabbit. If she's a house rabbit, place her cage in a quiet area away from the uproar. Make sure outdoor rabbits are confined safely away from the taunts of wild animals or neighborhood pets. Do your best to provide a relaxing, loving environment for your pet rabbit.

Geriatric Care

Aging is inevitable, and in time your youthful rabbit will reach her golden years. You might notice your normally playful rabbit becoming more sedate, or even a little stiff. Some aging rabbits lose a little weight. Such minor changes are a normal part of aging.

Provide an older rabbit with plenty of hay that is easy to reach.

Domestic rabbits live anywhere from five to ten years. When a rabbit is past five to six years old, she is considered geriatric.

There's no need to be alarmed by the changes that come with age as long as your rabbit is in good health. But you should be prepared to offer special help and be understanding of your elderly rabbit.

Many older rabbits become stiff with arthritis, especially in the hind legs. It may be more difficult for an older rabbit to hop in and out of her litter box or more difficult to reach up and pull hay from the hayrack. Minor modifications in the rabbit's living quarters can make life easier for the older rabbit. Cut down one side of the litter box for easier entry, lower the hayrack, and feed your rabbit on the floor so she doesn't have to reach into a bowl.

It can be more difficult for an older rabbit to clean herself. Daily brushing is essential to remove loose hair and keep the coat clean. Gentle touching and massage also feel good to older rabbits.

Older rabbits can develop problems with diarrhea or incontinence. If you notice a problem, don't assume it's just old age. Have the rabbit checked by a vet. If all is okay, realize it's a messy problem that requires a creative solution. Some rabbit owners put newborn-size baby diapers on their elderly rabbits!

Yearly health exams are especially important for an older rabbit, so make sure you make regular vet visits. A rabbit-savvy vet is able to discern between natural aging changes and disease. An older rabbit needs and deserves the best of care. Take time to make sure your older rabbit is comfortable and healthy. You won't regret it.

Emergency!

Emergency situations can arise quickly, and if you're not sure what to do, your rabbit can die. That's why rabbit experts urge beginners to be prepared for the worst-case scenario. Here's what you need to know.

Rabbits hide illnesses, which means that a rabbit can be very sick and an inexperienced rabbit owner may not know it—until it's too late. A healthy bunny is active, curious, and playful. A sick rabbit becomes quiet, may not want to eat or drink, or seems depressed. Her eyes may appear glassy, or she may breathe faster than usual. Learn to pay close attention to your rabbit and to learn what behaviors are normal for her. That way, you will notice right away if there's a change that could indicate illness.

A rabbit first aid kit is invaluable in an emergency.

Know ahead of time the rabbit-savvy vet you will contact in the event of an emergency. Post his or her telephone number (including an emergency number or pager number), address, and business hours by the telephone. Ask your rabbit vet to recommend a nearby emergency vet clinic as a backup. Know the route to both clinics and the estimated driving time.

Keep a bunny first aid kit on hand. You don't need a lot of items for your kit, but rabbit experts recommend having a heating pad or hot-water bottle for shock or hypothermia; styptic powder, gauze bandages, and sterile cotton pads for bleeding wounds; scissors to cut gauze; rubbing alcohol to cool an overheated rabbit; and a towel to wrap around the rabbit.

Learn how to assess a rabbit's vital signs so when you call the vet you can relay the information. Feel for the rabbit's pulse by placing a finger in the groin area or on the chest. (If the rabbit is in shock, her pulse may be very slow.) Check the rabbit's gum color, which is pink in a healthy rabbit. Bluish or pale gums are a sign of a circulation problem.

Keep the number of an
after-hours vet posted in
case of a late
night emergency.

Life-Threatening Emergencies

Some situations require immediate care to keep a rabbit alive. Generally, assume the following situations are life threatening and contact a vet immediately:

- Drowning
- Heatstroke
- Seizure or sudden neurological changes
- Poisoning
- Severe bleeding
- Unconsciousness

Other serious situations that may not be life threatening, but require that you call the vet right away are:

- Constipation (possible intestinal blockage)
- Maggots under the tail
- Minor bleeding wounds
- Minor burns (from chewing on electrical cords)
- Severe cold symptoms
- Watery diarrhea

Never hesitate to contact your vet with questions and concerns. Remember that it is always better to be overcautious when it comes to emergency situations.

CHAPTER SEVEN

Think Like
a Rabbit:
Rabbit Behavior

Domestic rabbits are similar physically and mentally to their wild ancestors. That's important to know if you wish to truly understand and happily live with your pet. First, remember that a domestic rabbit has the same sharp senses of a wild rabbit. A house bunny sees (though better in twilight), hears, and smells just about everything going on in your home: the kids running around, the ring of the doorbell, the smell of dinner cooking. An outdoor rabbit is acutely aware of goings-on outside the hutch. A rabbit's fabulous senses are his gift of protection against predators in the wild. Second, remember that a rabbit is a prey animal. His acute senses help him see, hear, and smell danger. Well-cared-for domestic rabbits need not be wary of predator threats, but instinctively they are. That's just the way rabbits are made. Whether living in the wild or sharing your home, a rabbit is extremely sensitive and easily frightened.

Owners must temper interactions with their pet rabbits in light of the rabbit's sensitive nature. That means you should speak softly to your pet. Handle him gently. Don't move quickly toward him, and never chase him. Keep noise to a minimum. Supervise interactions with other household pets. Avoid as best you can any situations in which your rabbit might feel threatened.

Wild rabbits are most active at dawn and dusk, which is when they usually venture out to look for food. Your pet rabbit is naturally most active at these times, too. He may wish to eat or be interested in exploring the house. Try to keep consistent with a rabbit's natural time clock by feeding and supervising outings at dawn or dusk. He may spend the rest of his day napping, so try to be respectful of his natural need for sleep.

Unneutered bucks may mount other rabbits.

Mating and raising a family is a normal part of a wild rabbit's life. The same instincts that prompt wild does and bucks to mate also prompt unneutered domestic rabbits to exhibit their own mating behaviors. There's nothing wrong with these instincts, of course, but they do manifest themselves in behaviors that can be annoying or problematic to owners. In fact, breeding behaviors present the largest source of problem behaviors in pet rabbits. Common mating behaviors include urine spraying (the buck marks his territory); crankiness toward an owner or digging (both are common in young does); mounting by the buck; and nipping, biting, scratching, or aggressive behavior, which can be common in bucks and does. In the wild, such behaviors are ways bucks and does communicate readiness or willingness to mate or ways they defend territory. For pet owners, they create frustration. After all, it's no fun to get nipped when you try to pick up your doe or to have to constantly clean and deodorize your house because your buck sprays.

You can't change nature, but you can alter it somewhat by having your rabbit spayed or neutered. Surgically altering your rabbit reduces negative mating behaviors, resulting in a better pet. Does and bucks should be altered before they become sexually mature. Neuter a male at three to four months and spay a female at four to six months to keep mating behaviors to a minimum.

The wild rabbit is fastidious, constantly cleaning himself and keeping his burrow clean. Pet rabbits are also naturally clean animals. If you notice that your rabbit is dirty, especially his rear end, it can mean trouble. Either you aren't keeping his cage or hutch clean or he is suffering from diarrhea.

Understanding a Rabbit's Language

Wild rabbits use sounds and body postures to communicate with each other in establishing a hierarchy in a colony, defending territory against intruders, and indicating a willingness to mate. Domesticated rabbits retain that ability to communicate, and they often do just that with their human owners. Something, however, is usually lost in the translation. For example, what does it mean when a rabbit rubs his chin against objects? Here are a few common ways rabbits "talk" via sounds and body language, followed by their generally accepted interpretations:

- Chin rubbing: Most common in males, rubbing with the underside of the chin establishes territory. A buck has scent glands under his chin, and when he rubs his chin on an object he leaves a scent detectable to other rabbits. When your rabbit rubs his chin against a couch or your hand, he's simply marking his turf.

- Ear shaking: Rabbits communicate being annoyed by shaking their ears.

- Flattened body: To make themselves less visible to predators, wild rabbits flatten their bodies against the ground with their ears held tightly against the head. This position, in wild or pet rabbits, means the animal is extremely frightened.

- Foot tapping: When a rabbit is afraid, he drums his foot to alert other family members to danger.

- Growling: Yes, rabbits growl; a short, barking growl can be heard when a rabbit feels aggressive.

- Licking: Rabbits lick each other and their owners to show affection.

- Purring: Purring by males is a sign they're ready to mate; purring, produced by chattering teeth, is also a sign of contentedness.

- Screaming: Rarely heard, but when it is the sound is hair-raising. Rabbits scream when deathly afraid, as when caught by a predator or in a trap. Screaming also indicates extreme pain when frightened.

- Sitting up: A curious and cautious rabbit puts his ears up and sits up on his haunches to look, listen,and smell for trouble.

- Spraying: Spraying urine, usually done by a buck, is a behavior used to mark territory.

For the best results, discipline a rabbit immediately when he's caught misbehaving and always be consistent.

Behavioral Problems

Believe it or not, the primary reason pet owners dump pets at animal shelters is because of behavioral problems. Unfortunately, rabbits are not exempt from being dumped because they can present owners with some natural-but-frustrating behaviors: chewing, biting, burrowing, scratching, sexual behaviors, and soiling the house. The key to dealing with these behaviors is to understand your rabbit. If you don't understand how Bunny thinks and why he does what he does, you probably won't be able to prevent or solve the problem. Remember, such behaviors are not problems to a rabbit. He does what comes naturally! For example, if you're frustrated and ready to call it quits on rabbit ownership because Bunny has gnawed away at your handsome oak furniture, don't punish him. Realize that a rabbit's teeth grow continuously. Rabbits must chew on something to keep their teeth worn down and in proper alignment.

For chewing, recognize that rabbits chew almost anything when the urge hits, including a wood hutch, electrical cords, books, furniture, or shoes. And young rabbits are especially crazy about chewing. The trick is to provide your rabbit with plenty of acceptable, rabbit-safe chew toys at all times and to confine your pet to a rabbit-proofed area. While you can never change a rabbit's need to chew, you can direct it away from expensive wood furniture and toward inexpensive, safe chew toys. Protect furniture and wires that can't be removed by covering them.

Burrowing is another natural rabbit habit. In pet rabbits, burrowing turns up as digging at carpets, flooring, or even digging a tunnel in the backyard. Supervision is the best way to prevent burrowing. Don't allow your rabbit access to favored areas such as the carpet, and be especially careful when taking your rabbit outdoors. Attach a harness and leash to your pet to prevent an escape, or confine him in an area he can't dig himself out of.

Getting scratched by a rabbit is no fun—it hurts. A rabbit's strong hind legs and sharp nails can inflict painful blows and scratches. Scratching can usually be prevented by properly handling your rabbit, though. A rabbit who feels uncomfortable or insecure while being handled is likely to kick out with those powerful legs. Be sure to handle your rabbit correctly so he feels secure, and for extra protection, wrap the rabbit in a towel and wear long sleeves before carrying him. In addition, keep your rabbit's nails trimmed short.

The best way to keep house soiling to a minimum is to litter box train your rabbit. Be aware that intact bucks and in-season does, even if they are litter trained, mark with urine if left unsupervised. Once areas are soiled, you must clean them thoroughly to discourage further marking.

Biting is one of the rabbit's defenses. A hurt, frightened, or irritated rabbit will nip, as will a rabbit who is not used to human contact. Handled properly, most rabbits do not bite or resort to this type of defensive behavior. Handling should begin when the rabbit is young, about eight to ten weeks old, and it should be done carefully and gently. Keep in mind that nipping can be a rabbit's way of saying, *I've had enough*. Take the hint and back off. Or, if you're reaching into the cage and get nipped, realize you may be invading territory. Open the door and let your rabbit come out on his own. Some enthusiasts recommend that owners squeal whenever their rabbit nips them so that he realizes he's inflicting pain; others suggest wearing gloves when handling compulsive biters.

Consider wearing gloves
when handling a biting rabbit.

Rabbits go through what we might call "teenage years." Rabbits younger than one year old are full of energy, extremely mischievous, and prone to excessive chewing and digging. Fortunately, they do grow out of this behavior and settle down.

Rabbits are great diggers. Make sure that your little "gardener" can't tunnel an escape out of his outdoor pen.

Save your furniture by providing your bunny with safe items to chew such as dried branches and toys.

CHAPTER EIGHT

The Facts of Life

You probably haven't given it much thought, but the fabulous, distinct, and numerous breeds of rabbits available today are the results of a great deal of thought by countless individuals—the results of careful planning. Healthy, handsome domestic rabbits don't just appear. They're bred—hopefully by an individual or a rabbit breeder who is knowledgeable, dedicated, and honest.

Perhaps you've had a taste of rabbit ownership and are interested in breeding rabbits. It's a common desire of many owners. You have one rabbit, wouldn't it be great to have two, then an entire family? Not necessarily. You see, breeding rabbits is much, much more than mating your doe with your friend's buck. It requires in-depth knowledge of rabbit husbandry, a touch of experience, genetic wisdom, and an ability to plan, be selective, and keep records. The road to becoming a successful rabbit breeder is filled with pitfalls, and inexperienced breeders make countless mistakes. That's why breeding rabbits isn't for just anyone—and it may or may not be a hobby for which you're well suited. There's much to learn. Following is a small sampling. Keep in mind this is not intended to be a thorough how-to discussion on breeding but a brief introduction. If you're really serious about breeding rabbits, consult with an experienced, reputable breeder, and get involved with the American Rabbit Breeders Association.

Sexing

Sexing is simply determining if a rabbit is male or female, which is incredibly important when breeding! It may sound silly, but there have been owners surprised to learn that Peter the Belgian hare is actually Patricia because they relied on someone else's word regarding the sex. A wise breeder checks to make sure a doe is a doe and a buck is a buck; he or she also checks for genital infections or physical abnormalities. If you want to find out if your rabbit is male or female, it's best to ask a breeder or a veterinarian to check for you. Sexing can be tricky because it requires proper handling and a trained eye.

Breeding

The usual mating for a buck and a doe is relatively uneventful. A doe is placed in a buck's cage, and, providing she is receptive, copulation takes only a few seconds. The doe raises her rear end, the buck mates with her, and he falls over backward or on his side. The doe is removed from the cage. Since a doe becomes fertile upon stimulation by a buck—a doe does not have a regular cycle

Have a breeder or veterinarian show you how to determine your rabbit's sex.

or go into heat—many breeders mate the pair again in six to eight hours. This is about the amount of time it takes for the eggs to descend. A second mating is believed to improve conception rate.

Once the doe is mated, she is returned to her own quarters to wait out the thirty-one or so days of gestation. Breeders mark the calendar and keep track of the time until the blessed event.

Pregnancy

Pregnancy can be detected ten to fourteen days after mating. Physical palpation is the most common and accurate way breeders determine if a doe is pregnant. Between the tenth and fourteenth day of gestation, the fetuses grow rapidly, making them detectable by touch to the experienced breeder.

The doe receives no special care prior to detection of her pregnancy. Once it's determined that a doe is pregnant, some breeders gradually increase her feed until two days before kindling (birth), then they decrease it.

154

It's important not to overfeed a doe before or during a pregnancy. Obesity can make kindling difficult and can make it difficult for the doe to become pregnant in the first place. Internal fat can build up around the fallopian tubes and block eggs from descending.

Around twenty-seven days after mating, the doe needs a nest box, a place in which she will give birth and care for her young. The nest box should be clean, well ventilated, dry, filled with nesting material, and not too big or too small. The American Rabbit Breeders Association recommends that a nest box be about 2 inches longer than the doe in sitting position and 2 inches wider than the doe in the same position. A doe will foul (urinate and defecate in) a nest box that is too large.

Breeding rabbits is a huge responsibility.

Kindling

Kits are usually born in the quiet of the night, thirty-one or so days after conception. The doe licks and cleans each kit as he or she is born, and then the doe eats the placenta. A wise breeder leaves the dam (a mother rabbit) to her business and doesn't disturb her. Disturbing the new mother can stress and frighten her and her young. The next day, the breeder checks the dam and litter and removes any kits born dead. There are usually two to twelve kits in a litter depending on the breed—small breeds have smaller litters than large breeds. Newborn rabbits are extremely helpless. They're born without much fur, their ability to move is limited, and their eyes and ears are closed.

Lactation

The dam produces milk suited especially for her growing youngsters. The first few days she supplies the young with a "first milk" that contains substances to protect the vulnerable kits from disease. Though blind and without hearing, the kits have a sharp sense of smell, which is how they find the doe's nipples: the kits smell the milk. The young rabbits nurse once or twice a day until they are weaned several weeks later. Lactating is demanding for the doe. Breeders must pay close attention to her to ensure that she is eating and drinking properly to keep up milk production and to prevent nursing problems.

Top left: Kits are born hairless and tiny.
Bottom left: These ten-day-old kits have grown some fur and can open their eyes.

Kits nurse for up to eight weeks of age.

Weaning

The young rabbits grow and thrive under the doe's care. Their eyes open at about ten days, and they're out of the nest box at three weeks of age. As soon as the youngsters are out and about, they can start nibbling on pellets. Weaning, the time to stop nursing and be separated from the doe, usually occurs at about eight weeks of age, sometimes later in large breeds. This, too, can be a stressful time period, and breeders take special care of the doe and young to prevent difficulties.

Why Breed?

Experienced breeders take much pride and joy in their rabbits. They're thrilled when a doe becomes pregnant and gives birth to a litter of healthy, beautiful rabbits. Though it requires planning, effort, and wisdom, it's worth it. There may be a champion-to-be in that next litter!

Realize, though, that responsible breeders don't just breed any rabbit at any time. Matings are studied, calculated, and planned to ensure that the next generation is true to breed standards and healthy. The goal is to improve, not just increase.

If you're interested in breeding your rabbit, good questions to consider are: Why? What are your goals? Do you hope to make money? Do you want more than one rabbit? Do you think the experience will be good for your children?

Now that you've thought for a moment, let's address some issues: don't expect to make money breeding any kind of animal. Contrary to popular belief, responsible breeding simply is not a money-making process. It requires money! Anyway, experienced, responsible breeders don't do it for money. Most breeders are just crazy about rabbits. They're devoted to the species or a particular breed. Their efforts are labors of love.

If you're breeding because you want another rabbit, buy one from a reputable breeder or adopt one from a shelter. It's that simple. Breeding your doe may result in a litter of eight or so rabbits. Unless you plan to keep all of them (which would result in even more rabbits if they are not neutered), what do you plan to do with the remaining seven?

Children benefit from learning about rabbits, including how they're born, but that doesn't mean you have to turn your pet into a science project. Check out a book from the library, ask a rabbit breeder to give your child a tour of a rabbitry, or watch a nature video together.

If you're really serious about breeding, consult with an experienced breeder and get involved with the American Rabbit Breeders Association.

A Better Alternative

Why all the discouraging talk about breeding? Why not mate your rabbit right away? Well, there's a big problem in the rabbit world that gets little attention: overpopulation. Shelters are filled with unwanted and abandoned rabbits. Following cats and dogs, rabbits are the most common animals in shelters. There are too

These Netherland dwarf
bunnies are all from the
same litter and need
loving homes.

many rabbits and not enough homes. Many births are the results of careless breeding or unplanned matings, perhaps by a well-meaning owner, such as yourself, who was interested in breeding. The best advice is to give up the notion of breeding. Spay or neuter your pet rabbit, and leave breeding to the responsible breeder.

CHAPTER NINE

Just for Fun

Okay, now the fun begins! You've purchased supplies, prepared your home, and read a stack of rabbit books. Finally, it's time to enjoy living with your new pet rabbit. Perhaps you're unsure about what you can do with Bunny, though. You know you must feed and groom him and clean up after him. Is there anything else? You bet there is. Read on to learn more.

Showing

Welcome to the wonderful world of rabbit shows! Showing is a favorite activity of many rabbit enthusiasts who say it's a fun, interesting, and challenging hobby. Showing is a great way to learn about rabbits or particular breeds, and it's a great way to meet others who share an interest in rabbits. Unfortunately, rabbit showing is not well publicized, probably because it's more of a participant activity rather than a spectator sport. But publicized or not, it's extremely popular with rabbit enthusiasts.

All rabbit shows are fun, but some are more serious than others are. Shows sponsored by the American Rabbit Breeders Association (ARBA), the international organization that sanctions shows and registers animals, attract the serious-minded breeder or enthusiast. Rabbits entered in ARBA shows are judged against a description (set forth by the ARBA) called the Standard of Perfection—a physical description of an ideal specimen of each recognized breed, including size, shape, color, weight, and other specifications. The goal of many serious breeders is to produce rabbits who come as close as possible to the Standard of Perfection and to earn recognition for those rabbits at shows.

Can any rabbit be entered in an ARBA show? Only purebreds need apply here. Show rabbits can be registered, which ensures that a rabbit is a purebred, but registration is not required to compete. (A three-generation pedigree is required to be registered.) A rabbit must be show quality to earn recognition, or, ultimately, the prestigious title of Grand Champion. Not all purebreds are show quality, though they may be perfectly wonderful rabbits. A show-quality rabbit displays the best characteristics of his breed and comes close to the written standard.

The ARBA requires that all rabbits be tattooed in the left ear with a legible, permanent identification number, usually the registration number, before they can be shown. This is usually done before the show by breeders or a licensed show registrar.

Serious rabbit enthusiasts of all ages can compete in ARBA shows. Shows offer open categories (all ages) or youth categories

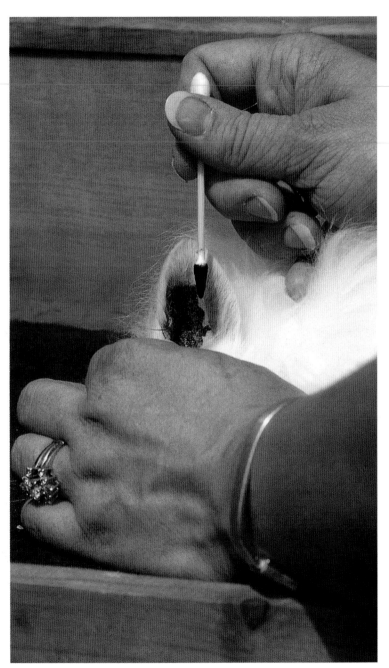

Before your rabbit gets tattooed for a show, the ink is swabbed onto the left ear.

(for ages nineteen or younger). Shows are located throughout the U.S. and are often hosted by regional rabbit clubs. Rabbits are judged by ARBA judges, who must undergo rigorous study and testing before being licensed by the organization.

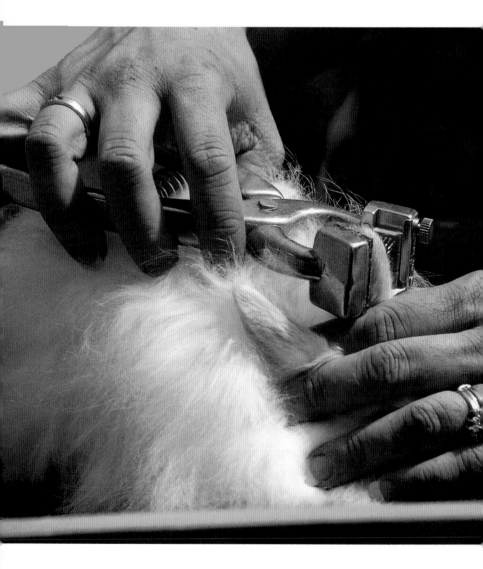

If you're interested in serious showing, start by joining the ARBA (you must be a member to register a rabbit). Then locate an experienced breeder or show competitor who can help you find a show-quality rabbit and help you learn the ropes.

After the ink is applied, then the ear is stamped to permanently imprint an identification number.

For children, 4-H rabbit projects, sponsored by the U.S. Department of Agriculture-Maintained 4-H Youth Program, are another route to showing. Open to children aged nine through nineteen, the usual 4-H rabbit project teaches youngsters proper rabbit care, handling, feeding, and grooming. Exhibiting is often part of the program. Aiming to educate and encourage young members, 4-H is a wonderful and fun way to introduce children to the world of rabbits.

Clubs such as 4-H help young members learn how to responsibly care for and show rabbits in a fun and structured environment.

Ten Steps to Serious Showing

1. Join the ARBA.

2. Acquire (and register, if you choose) a show-quality rabbit.

3. Have the rabbit's left ear tattooed with an identification number.

4. Look up an upcoming show in Domestic Rabbits, the ARBA publication that lists all upcoming ARBA-sanctioned shows by date and state.

5. Contact the show secretary of the show you'd like to attend,and request a show catalog.

6. Fill out the entry form and return it before the entry deadline. Keep a copy of the entry form.

7. Arrive at the show early and check in with the show secretary.

8. Wait for your class to be called.

9. Do last minute grooming touch-ups.

10. Hope for the best, and let Bunny do the rest!

There are 4-H rabbit shows held throughout the country; attend your county fair this year and you're likely to see one. Participants follow the same rules and breed standards found at ARBA shows. Many 4-H members show purebred rabbits, but mixed-breed rabbits are welcome in a special showmanship class. In this class, young exhibitors demonstrate their knowledge of rabbit anatomy, care, and proper handling. The 4-H projects are staffed by dedicated volunteers, usually parents and rabbit enthusiasts with a desire to share their love for rabbits with children.

Since 4-H clubs are administered by the county extension services in each state, you must contact the county extension office for information on local rabbit projects. Regardless of how serious your goals are, showing is an exciting and enjoyable way to have fun with your new pet rabbit, and it doesn't require a lot of preparation for the rabbit, either. Proper feeding, fresh water, clean quarters, and periodic grooming are all you need to present a winning specimen to the judge.

Playtime

Organized, formal activities such as showing are great, but another wonderful way to have fun with your rabbit is to grab a few toys and invent a game. Rabbits are playful creatures and have been known to play with their human owners and with other household pets. Rabbits will chase a toy, bat a ball, or pick up a paper plate (using the mouth) and toss it. Given the rabbit's timid, prey-animal nature, it's best to provide the toys and let your rabbit start the game. Don't try to force a game, or you might frighten your rabbit. For example, place an empty paper towel roll right in front of Bunny. Give the roll a nudge, then sit back and wait to see what happens. Or roll a ball inside a paper bag. The rabbit's curious nature will drive him to investigate—and it won't be long before the playing begins.

Experienced owners understand how much rabbits enjoy playing, so they keep their pets occupied with safe, interesting toys. Providing toys helps eliminate boredom, which in turn keeps destructive behaviors to a minimum. Playing encourages exercise to keep the rabbit physically fit.

You can make toys from items already in your home—paper plates, paper bags, and paper towel rolls—or you can purchase ready-made rabbit or cat toys. Rotate toys to keep them new to your rabbit, and supervise playtime to make sure the rabbit doesn't ingest something he shouldn't.

Simple Toy Ideas

- A cardboard box to hide in or hop over
- A paper plate to toss in the air
- An empty frozen juice can to roll
- A safe fruit tree branch to chew
- An empty cereal box or cooked oats container to nudge
- A paper bag to crawl inside

Rabbits seem to enjoy chasing balls.

Companionship

As you grow to understand your pet rabbit and become aware of his individual personality, you will probably come to realize what a special companion you have. The basis for enjoying and having fun with your pet rabbit is to appreciate the simple daily activities you share.

For example, feeding your rabbit need not be a boring task but a special time in which you serve up a nutritious feast for a friend. Gentle petting, even if it's a grooming chore, is comforting to both you and your bunny. Cage cleaning is a labor of love. Trips to the vet are a service that keeps a small friend healthy and comfortable.

It's really how you look at your relationship that determines your enjoyment level. Cultivate a positive attitude and you'll find that no matter what you do with your bunny friend, it's fun!

Appendix

THINK OF THE END OF THIS BOOK AS THE BEGINNING of an adventure starring you and your rabbit friend. New discoveries about the rabbit species, and yourself, await you as you grow into the role of responsible rabbit owner. Everyone needs support and help to be their best, though, so following is a list of resources. Included are books, publications, organizations, and associations that can help you be the best rabbit owner possible. Whenever you have questions, problems, or difficulties, be sure to ask for help. Enjoy!

Organizations and Associations

American Holistic Veterinary Medical Association
2218 Old Emmorton Road
Bel Air, MD 21015
(410) 569-0795
www.ahvma.org
office@ahvma.org
Dedicated to encouraging the alternative approaches to veterinary medicine. Check the website for a listing of holistic veterinarians in your area.

American Humane Association
63 Inverness Drive East
Englewood, CO 80112
(303) 792-9900
www.americanhumane.org
National animal welfare organization.

American Rabbit Breeders Association, Inc.
P.O. Box 5667
Bloomington, IL 61702
(309) 664-7500
www.arba.net
arbapost@aol.com
Member organization dedicated to providing proper information on the raising and exhibition of rabbits and cavies.
Free brochures on rabbit and cavy care, breeding, feeding,
and showing available upon request, as well as referrals to
local clubs (two thousand nationwide). Yearly dues: $15.

American Veterinary Medical Association
1931 N. Meacham Road
Ste. 100
Schaumburg, IL 60173-4360
(847) 925-8070
www.avma.org
avmainfo@avma.org
Dedicated to advancing the science and art of veterinary
medicine. Encourages owners to discuss pet-care needs with
veterinarians, but has free online brochures on topics such
as vaccines, traveling with pets, and diseases.

House Rabbit Society

148 Broadway, Richmond, CA 94804

(510) 970-7575

membership@rabbit.org

www.rabbit.org

Member organization dedicated to rescuing and caring for rabbits. Rabbit care brochures and seminars. Yearly dues: $25.

National 4-H Council

7100 Connecticut Avenue

Chevy Chase, MD 20815

(301) 961-2800

www.4-h.org

Books

The ARBA Official Guidebook to Raising Better Rabbits and Cavies. American Rabbit Breeders Association, Inc., 1996.

Bennett, Bob. *Rabbits as a Hobby.* TFH, 1991.

Fraser, Samantha. *Hop to It: A Guide to Training Your Pet Rabbit.* Barron's Educational Series, 1991.

Harriman, Marinell. *The House Rabbit Handbook.* Drollery Press, 1995.

Mays, Marianne. *Pet Owner's Guide to Rabbits.* Howell Book House, 1995.

Pavia, Audrey. *Rabbits for Dummies.* Wiley Publishing 2003.

Pinney, Chris, D.V.M. *The Illustrated Veterinary Guide for Dogs, Cats, Birds and Exotic Pets.* McGraw-Hill, 2000.

Robinson, David. *Encyclopedia of Pet Rabbits.* TFH, 1979.

Siino, SiKora Betsy. *The Essential Rabbit.* Howell Book House, 1996.

Wegler, Monika. *Rabbits: A Complete Pet Owner's Manual.* Barron's Educational Series, 1999.

Magazines

House Rabbit Journal
House Rabbit Society
148 Broadway
Richmond, CA 94804
(510) 970-7575
www.rabbit.org

Glossary

alter: to spay or neuter a rabbit

breed: a distinct group of animals descended from common ancestors with similar characteristics, including color, shape, and size

buck: an adult male rabbit

coprophagy: an act in which a rabbit ingests its own soft fecal matter to receive nutrients

dam: the mother of a litter

dewlap: a pendulous fold of skin that hangs from the throat (more prominent in does)

doe: an adult female rabbit

gestation: the length of time between conception and kindling lasting approximately thirty-one days

hutch: a house for rabbits

kindle: to give birth

kindling: the process of giving birth to rabbits

kit: a newborn and very young rabbit

litter: the group of kits born to a doe

molt: to shed or grow fur

nest box: a warm, safe box that provides a rabbit with security. It also gives the doe a private area to kindle.

neuter: to surgically remove the testes from a male animal or the ovaries from a female

pedigree: a registry recording a line of ancestors of three generations or more

purebred: a pedigreed member of a recognized rabbit breed

rabbitry: a place where domestic rabbits are kept

registration: official examination and recording of a rabbit pedigree by a purebred rabbit registry such as the American Rabbit Breeders Association

selective breeding: breeding to encourage specific traits such as size or coat color

spay: to surgically remove the ovaries of a female animal

sire: the father of a litter

standard: written description of a purebred rabbit

undercoat: a growth of short hair or fur often hidden by a coat of longer hairs on an animal's body

wool: the soft, fleecy hair on Angora, American fuzzy lop, and Jersey wooly rabbits. The guard hairs and underfur resemble fine wool in texture.

Index

A
acquiring/choosing a rabbit
    from an individual, 55–57
    from breeders, 49–50
    breeds, 34–38
    considerations for commitment, 28, 32–34
    male versus female, 44
    personalities, 57
    personality, 40
    from a pet store, 52
    physical characteristics, 43–44
    from shelters, 5
    size, 40, 43
activity periods, 33
aging, 132–133
altering, 44, 85, 118–119, 141
American Rabbit Breeders Association (ARBA) shows. *See* showing
Angora rabbits, 15, 96
arthritis, 133
associations. *See* organizations/associations

B
bathing, 99
beginners, tips for, 47
behavior
    biting, 146
    burrowing, 145–146
    chewing, 145
    chin rubbing, 142
    coprophagy, 23
    digging, 20
    flattening the body, 142–143
    foot tapping, 143
    mating, 141
    problems, 145–146
    self-grooming, 23
    understanding, 106
    urine spraying, 143
    of wild rabbits, 20–21
birds, 82
biting, 146

bleeding, 137
books/magazines about rabbits, 11, 177–178
breeders, 49–50, 51
breeding
    alternatives to, 160–161
    for food, 14–15
    for fur, 15–16
    general issues of, 151–152
    kindling, 155, 157
    lactation, 157
    mating process, 152–153
    pregnancy, 153–154
    reasons for, 158–159
    sexing, 152
    weaning, 158
breeds
    choosing, 34–38
    development of, 15–16
    recognized, 34
    sizes, 40, 43
    temperaments/personalities, 40
burns, 137
burrowing, 145–146

C
cages, 63–68, 104–105. *See also* hutches
calciuria (bladder stones), 129
cats, 82
checking for health problems, 97
chewing, 71–72, 96, 145
chew sticks, 77
children, 33, 88–89, 159, 168–171
chin rubbing, 142
choosing a rabbit. *See* acquiring/choosing a rabbit
cleanliness, 116
cleanup, 104–105
clubs. *See* organizations/associations
coccidiosis, 129
colonies, 20, 24
communication, 23, 142–143
companionship, 173
constipation, 137
coprophagy, 23